THE ILLUSTRATED
FAMILY HYMN BOOK

THE ILLUSTRATED
FAMILY HYMN BOOK

Edited by Tony Jasper

A London Editions Book

THE SEABURY PRESS
NEW YORK

For
Jack Elliott and Alice Mathews

First published in 1980 by The Seabury Press, 815 Second Avenue,
New York, N.Y. 10017 and G. Schirmer Incorporated, 866 Third Avenue,
New York, N.Y. 10022.

This book
©1980 Tony Jasper and London Editions

Copyright holders for the music, lyrics and illustrations
as specified on pages 190-192

Library of Congress Catalog Card Number 79-92731

ISBN 0-8164-2051-3PBK
     0-8164-0413-8

This book was designed and produced in Great Britain
by London Editions Limited,
9 Long Acre, London WC2E 9LH.

Printed in Great Britain

Contents

Editor's Preface

For the most part this is a selection of popular hymns. Within this circumscribed field we have tried to take care that the basic truths of Christian faith have been stated. We have also tried to include a few hymns which celebrate the major Church festivals and general seasons of the year. The term 'popular' is often interpreted as, 'something liked by many people'. We would prefer to see popularity as meaning, in the context of this collection, material which has been seen to be true and reflective of Christian expression and the way people feel. Certain hymns are sung more than others because they speak more powerfully: truths about God, truths about ourselves and our responses.

The selection of the so-called 'popular' hymns has been influenced not only by the results of consultations with people involved in hymnology, but also by scanning a seemingly endless flow of hymn and songbooks, finding out the most requested hymns in radio and television programmes and by being aware of the various polls which have been conducted from time to time by religious denominations and the media in general.

One of the greatest problems in compilation has concerned the question of tune. Hymn lovers across the world may share a common appreciation for most of the titles found in this collection but in some cases this is confined to the lyric. Different tunes have assumed general consent in respective countries. It has left the difficult task of deciding which tune should find place here. The problem can be seen for instance in considering which tune should be used for *All Hail the Power, Love Divine* and *Praise, My Soul, the King of Heaven. All Hail the Power* has at least three tunes and these are known as 'Miles Lane' (or 'Coronation'), 'Diadem' and 'Ladywell'. We believe the first is known and used by more Christian groups than the others and so it has been chosen. It also commended itself on historical grounds since it was intrinsically associated with the lyric from the time of the first verse making its appearance in the *Gospel Magazine,* November 1779.

A whole host of tunes have been music for Charles Wesley's *Love Divine.* The *British Methodist Hymn Book* of 1932 with its additional *Hymns and Songs* published in 1969, officially gives three, but several others are in known use by British Methodists. The American, *Armed Forces Hymnal* gives further tunes and from consideration of other volumes it seems that the possible list is long. We chose 'Hyfrydol' because this tune is known and does find some use amongst virtually all Christian denominations. *Praise, My Soul, the King of Heaven* has two main tunes, 'Praise, My Soul' and 'Regent's Square'. We chose the second because it is known in most Christian circles even though there is ardent support for the first in some communions. This method of choice has been the one most commonly used in the final selection for a number of other hymns.

In terms of hymn composition and general advice a particular word of thanks must go to Albert M. Jakeway of the Methodist Publishing House, London, to Joyce Horn of the Oxford University Press, Peter H. Mundy, Raymond Short, Norman Goldhawk, to Warren Danskin and Bob Thompson of the American Church in London and to Paul Inwood who took care of the musical scores. Not least, thanks are due to the many talented artists who have made this volume so distinctive.

Tony Jasper, June 1979

Introduction

It is surprising that hymns, as we know them in the context of Christian worship, are a fairly recent innovation. It was not until the eighteenth century that they began to replace the solemnities of psalm chanting, although of course psalms are still in popular use in various Christian communities.

There is no agreement as to exactly how many hymns have been written. Estimates vary by millions but a mid-way figure between the claims which have been made would suggest five million. They appear in over 200 languages. Denominational hymn books contain only a fraction of the material that has been written.

The man who is acknowledged for the rise in popularity of hymns is Isaac Watts. He has been termed the real founder of English Hymnody. The main bulk of his published works appeared between 1706 and 1719. Another prominent name is Charles Wesley. In 1738, when during Whitsuntide he and brother John felt they were recipients of the Spirit, he wrote the first hymns of the Evangelical Revival.

Charles Wesley is associated with Methodism and the Methodists more than any other Christian Church have popularised the hymn. Certainly it is claimed by Methodists that Methodism was born in song. Wesley wrote over 6,500 hymns and many of them have found their way into the hymn books of the various Christian denominations.

In 1779 Wesley prefaced a collection of his own hymns by saying that their purpose was to raise and quicken the spirit of devotion, to confirm a person's faith, to enliven his hope, stirring and increasing his love to God and man. Few would disagree that such a statement is expressive of most hymn collections.

Since the time of Watts and Wesley there have been various moments which have precipitated an unusually large number of new songs and hymns. One example is the rise to popularity of the gospel song at the time of the revival missions of American evangelist Daniel L. Moody and his mission soloist Ira D. Sankey. The popular hymns of their late nineteenth century campaigns were gathered together in a collection which is popular still, *Sacred Songs and Solos*. Many of these were penned by the blind Fanny J. Crosby. She wrote at least 8,000 hymns. A number of songs in our collection represent that era and they include *Tell Me the Old, Old, Story, To God Be the Glory* and *Blessed Assurance*. These, and others of similar nature, received fresh popularity through Billy Graham's massive, worldwide, evangelistic campaigns during the 1950s and after. Graham, like Moody, had his own soloist and this was Beverly Shea; and he made generally known the song *How Great Thou Art*. It is found in this collection.

With the dawning of the twentieth century it was evident that it was necessary that hymnody should contain material reflective of a new time and a changing world. Yet there have been few hymns and songs that have become accepted. New tunes have often replaced the traditional but good contemporary lyrics have been in short supply. Few modern hymns have had lyrics which have expressed the Lordship of Christ against a technological-scientific backcloth. One of the best is found in this collection and this is *God of Concrete, God of Steel.*

Much contemporary material has caused confusion for the compilers of modern denominational hymn books. They remain uncertain whether some of the material which has come from a flourish of hymn writing in the 1960s will find a permanent place in congregational worship. Some of this has had a folk and rock background and been popularised through energetic young people's Christian movements, where the electric guitar has not been seen as synonymous with the devil. Many folk-rock, Christian recording artists and choirs have included this material on their albums. Whatever the pros and cons for the inclusion of these in denominational hymn books, several examples do find their way into this selection. They include *Presence of the Lord, Thank You* and *Jesus the Lord Said.*

While church hymn committees have deliberated there has been no lack of small groups and individuals who have busied themselves in publishing their own collections. The 1970s have seen a surfeit of material. Yet despite the value of these many publications there is still an important place for hymns which are timeless. It is irrelevant whether they stem from the fourteenth or nineteenth centuries.

Hymns, of course, are not just for church-going people. They have received general acceptance. Radio and television have helped some hymns to have the popularity of pop songs. The BBC in London, has estimated that 60 million people regularly listen to their Sunday evening programme, *Sunday Half-Hour,* which is broadcast on home and BBC World Service which is networked to over 50 countries and has run without break since 1941. Each week it comes from a different location — prisons, schools, service bases, churches of all denominations and mission halls take part and show clearly how hymn-singing attracts all kinds and conditions of men and women. The BBC also weekly broadcasts a television programme of hymn singing which has attracted a high proportion of the British population as its viewing audience.

It does not seem an outrageous claim to suggest that the hymn unites the peoples of the world.

FOR THE LORD GOD IS A SUN AND SHIELD: THE LORD WILL GIVE GRACE AND GLORY: NO GOOD THING WILL HE WITHHOLD FROM THEM THAT WALK UPRIGHTLY.

PS. LXXXIV 11.

Abide with Me

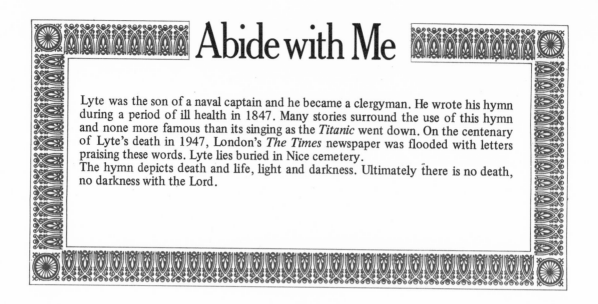

Lyte was the son of a naval captain and he became a clergyman. He wrote his hymn during a period of ill health in 1847. Many stories surround the use of this hymn and none more famous than its singing as the *Titanic* went down. On the centenary of Lyte's death in 1947, London's *The Times* newspaper was flooded with letters praising these words. Lyte lies buried in Nice cemetery.

The hymn depicts death and life, light and darkness. Ultimately there is no death, no darkness with the Lord.

Eventide

W. H. Monk 1823-89

1 A - bide with me; fast falls the e - ven - tide; the dark - ness deep - ens;
Lord, with me a - bide; when o - ther help - ers fail, and com - forts
flee, help of the help - less, oh, a - bide with me.

2 Swift to its close ebbs out life's little day;
　earth's joys go dim, its glories pass away;
　change and decay in all around I see:
　O thou who changest not, abide with me!

3 I need thy presence every passing hour;
　what but thy grace can foil the tempter's power?
　Who like thyself my guide and stay can be?
　Through cloud and sunshine, oh, abide with me.

4 I fear no foe, with thee at hand to bless;
　ills have no weight, and tears no bitterness;
　where is death's sting? where, grave, thy victory?
　I triumph still if thou abide with me.

5 Hold thou thy cross before my closing eyes,
　shine through the gloom, and point me to the skies;
　heaven's morning breaks, and earth's vain shadows flee:
　in life, in death, O Lord, abide with me!

Henry Francis Lyte 1793-1847

All Glory, Laud and Honour

St Theodulf of Orleans wrote his words when imprisoned in the cloisters of Angers, France. His original version had 78 lines and contained numerous references to the parishes of Angers.

Although sung at other times this hymn has become mandatory for Palm Sunday. It captures the spontaneous joy which greeted the King of Kings as he rode into Jerusalem. Its use of 'palm' follows the Biblical version of John's Gospel since in both Matthew and Mark the crowd use branches from the trees.

St Theodulph

M. Teschner 1584-1635

REFRAIN

1 All glo - ry, laud and hon - our to thee, Re - deem - er, King, to

whom the lips of chil - dren made sweet ho - san - nas ring!

2 Thou art the King of Is - rael, thou Da - vid's roy - al

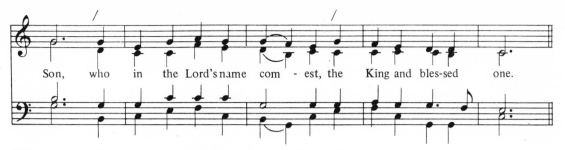

Son, who in the Lord's name com - est, the King and bles-sed one.

(The refrain (v. 1) is sung at the beginning and after each verse)

3 The company of angels
  are praising thee on high,
  and mortal men and all things
  created make reply.

4 The people of the Hebrews
  with palms before thee went;
  our praise, and prayer, and anthems
  before thee we present.

5 To thee before thy passion
  they sang their hymns of praise;
  to thee, now high exalted,
  our melody we raise.

6 Thou didst accept their praises;
  accept the prayers we bring,
  who in all good delightest,
  thou good and gracious King.

Theodulf of Orleans c. 750-821
tr. John Mason Neale 1818-66

All Hail the Power

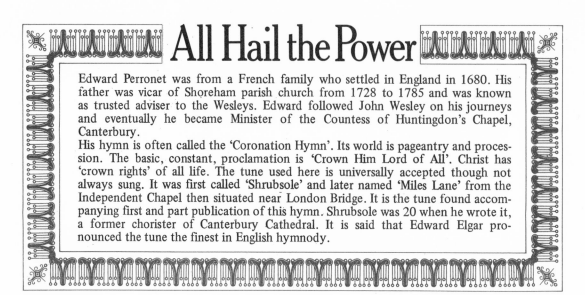

Edward Perronet was from a French family who settled in England in 1680. His father was vicar of Shoreham parish church from 1728 to 1785 and was known as trusted adviser to the Wesleys. Edward followed John Wesley on his journeys and eventually he became Minister of the Countess of Huntingdon's Chapel, Canterbury.

His hymn is often called the 'Coronation Hymn'. Its world is pageantry and procession. The basic, constant, proclamation is 'Crown Him Lord of All'. Christ has 'crown rights' of all life. The tune used here is universally accepted though not always sung. It was first called 'Shrubsole' and later named 'Miles Lane' from the Independent Chapel then situated near London Bridge. It is the tune found accompanying first and part publication of this hymn. Shrubsole was 20 when he wrote it, a former chorister of Canterbury Cathedral. It is said that Edward Elgar pronounced the tune the finest in English hymnody.

Miles Lane

W. Shrubsole 1760-1806

1 All hail the pow'r of Je-sus' name; let an-gels pros-trate fall; bring forth the roy-al di-a-dem to crown him, crown him, crown him, crown him, Lord of all.

made their glow-ing co - lours, he made their ti-ny wings.

(The refrain (v. 1) is sung at the beginning and after each verse)

3 The purple-headed mountain,
the river running by,
the sunset, and the morning
that brightens up the sky.

4 The cold wind in the winter,
the pleasant summer sun,
the ripe fruits in the garden,
he made them every one.

5 He gave us eyes to see them,
and lips, that we might tell
how great is God almighty,
who has made all things well.

Cecil Frances Alexander
1823-95

Amazing Grace

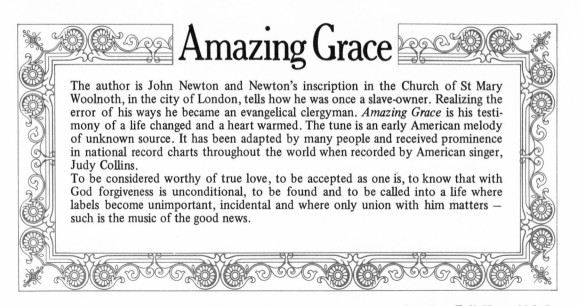

The author is John Newton and Newton's inscription in the Church of St Mary Woolnoth, in the city of London, tells how he was once a slave-owner. Realizing the error of his ways he became an evangelical clergyman. *Amazing Grace* is his testimony of a life changed and a heart warmed. The tune is an early American melody of unknown source. It has been adapted by many people and received prominence in national record charts throughout the world when recorded by American singer, Judy Collins.

To be considered worthy of true love, to be accepted as one is, to know that with God forgiveness is unconditional, to be found and to be called into a life where labels become unimportant, incidental and where only union with him matters — such is the music of the good news.

American Folk Hymn Melody
arr. E. O. Excell 1851-1921

Amazing Grace

1 A - maz - ing grace (how sweet the sound) that saved a
wretch like me! I once was lost, but
now am found, was blind, but now I see.

2 'Twas grace that taught my heart to fear,
and grace my fears relieved;
how precious did that grace appear
the hour I first believed!

3 Through many dangers, toils and snares
I have already come:
'tis grace has brought me safe thus far,
and grace will lead me home.

4 The Lord has promised good to me,
his word my hope secures;
he will my shield and portion be
as long as life endures.

John Newton 1725-1807

And Can It Be

This is one of Wesley's finest hymns. It expresses the utter joy and freedom which come from the conversion experience. Wesley marvels why God in Christ should die for him. In the face of such love he is overwhelmed. On the last Sunday afternoon of his life, as he lay on his death-bed, a friend repeated to him the last two lines of this hymn. Wesley replied, ' 'Tis enough, he, our precious Emmanuel, has purchased, has promised all.'

Sagina

T. Campbell 1825

1 And can it be that I should gain an in - t'rest in the Sa - viour's blood?

Died he for me, who caus'd his pain? for me, who him to death pur-sued?

A - maz-ing love! How can it be that thou, my God, should'st die for me!

maz-ing love! How can it be that thou, my God, shoud'st die for me!

A -maz-ing love! How can it be that thou, my God, should'st die for me!

2 'Tis mystery all! The Immortal dies:
who can explore his strange design?
In vain the first-born seraph tries
to sound the depths of love divine.
'Tis mercy all! Let earth adore,
let angel minds inquire no more.

3 He left his Father's throne above —
so free, so infinite his grace —
emptied himself of all but love,
and bled for Adam's helpless race.
'Tis mercy all, immense and free;
for, O my God, it found out me!

4 Long my imprisoned spirit lay
fast bound in sin and nature's night;
thine eye diffused a quickening ray —
I woke, the dungeon flamed with light;
my chains fell off, my heart was free,
I rose, went forth, and followed thee.

5 No condemnation now I dread;
Jesus, and all in him, is mine!
Alive in him, my living head,
and clothed in righteousness divine,
bold I approach the eternal throne,
and claim the crown, through Christ, my own.

Charles Wesley 1707-88

Blessed Assurance

This is one of the most popular hymns associated with the revival campaigns of the nineteenth century. It has continued to hold a high place in the affections of many Christians. In more recent time it featured as one of the most frequently sung hyms at the Billy Graham campaign meetings. Its writer Fanny Crosby was from New York. She lost her sight when only six weeks old. She trained as a teacher and married a blind musician Alexander van Alstyne. It is estimated she wrote over 2,000 hymns. Many of these can be found in popular collections like *Golden Bells*, *Redemption Hymnal* and *Sacred Songs and Solos*.

This Gospel hymn speaks of personal blessing and assurance. It tells the story of what Jesus the Saviour means to a believer. And that is everything, it is like heaven.

Blessed Assurance

J. F. Knapp 1839-1908

Bles-sed as - sur - ance, Je-sus is mine: oh, what a fore - taste of glo - ry di -

vine! Heir of sal - va-tion, pur-chase of God; born of his Spi - rit, wash'd in his blood.

REFRAIN

This is my sto - ry, this is my song, prais - ing my Sa - viour all the day

long; this is my sto - ry, this is my song, prais-ing my Sa- viour all the day long.

(The refrain is sung after each verse)

2 Perfect submission, perfect delight,
   visions of rapture burst on my sight;
   angels descending, bring from above
   echoes of mercy, whispers of love.

3 Perfect submission, all is at rest,
   I in my Saviour am happy and blest;
   watching and waiting, looking above,
   filled with his goodness, lost in his love.

Frances Jane van Alstyne 1820-1915

Christ the Lord Is Risen To-Day

This has become an essential choice on Easter Sunday whatever the Christian communion. The version here includes the line change made by Martin Madan for his 1760 *Psalms and Hymns* collection for he replaced 'Dying once, he all doth save' with 'Once he died our souls to save'.

Each verse ends with repeated cry of 'Hallelujah' and this use has a long and celebrated history. It was an old Christian custom to shout this word on an Easter morning. Wesley's hymn speaks of victory and in this is found life which transcends death.

Easter Morn

Lyra Davidica 1708

1 Christ the Lord is ris'n to day; Hal - le - lu - jah!
sons of men and an - gels say: Hal - le - lu - jah!
raise your joys and tri - umphs high: Hal - le - lu - jah!

26

sing, ye heav'ns; thou earth, re-ply: *Hal - le - lu - jah!*

(Hallelujah is sung at the end of every line)

2 Love's redeeming work is done;
 fought the fight, the battle won:
 vain the stone, the watch, the seal;
 Christ hath burst the gates of hell:

3 Lives again our glorious King;
 where, O death, is now thy sting?
 Once he died our souls to save:
 where's thy victory, boasting grave?

4 Soar we now where Christ hath led,
 following our exalted head:
 made like him, like him we rise;
 ours the cross, the grave, the skies:

5 King of glory! Soul of bliss!
 Everlasting life is this,
 thee to know, thy power to prove,
 thus to sing, and thus to love:

Charles Wesley 1707-88

Come Down O Love Divine

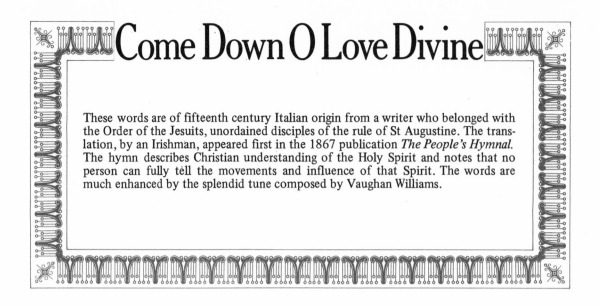

These words are of fifteenth century Italian origin from a writer who belonged with the Order of the Jesuits, unordained disciples of the rule of St Augustine. The translation, by an Irishman, appeared first in the 1867 publication *The People's Hymnal.* The hymn describes Christian understanding of the Holy Spirit and notes that no person can fully tell the movements and influence of that Spirit. The words are much enhanced by the splendid tune composed by Vaughan Williams.

Down Ampney

Ralph Vaughan Williams 1872-1958

1 Come down, O Love di - vine, seek thou this soul of mine, and vi - sit it with thine own ar - dour glow - ing; O Com-fort-er, draw near, with - in my heart ap - pear, and kind-le it, thy ho - ly flame be - stow - ing.

2 Oh, let it freely burn,
   till earthly passions turn
   to dust and ashes, in its heat consuming;
   and let thy glorious light
   shine ever on my sight,
   and clothe me round, the while my path illuming.

3 Let holy charity
   mine outward vesture be,
   and lowliness become mine inner clothing;
   true lowliness of heart,
   which takes the humbler part,
   and o'er its own shortcomings weeps with loathing.

4 And so the yearning strong,
   with which the soul will long,
   shall far outpass the power of human telling;
   for none can guess its grace,
   till he become the place
   wherein the Holy Spirit make his dwelling.

Bianco da Siena *d*. 1434
tr. Richard Frederick Littledale 1833-90

The Holy Ghost sent, Acts. 2°.

29

Come, Ye Thankful People, Come

This first appeared in *Psalms and Hymns,* 1844. It has become an essential part of any Harvest Festival gathering. Alford was Dean at Canterbury Cathedral in England from 1857 to 1871 and thus occupied an important spiritual position at what is the cradle of Christianity for English speaking peoples. He died at Canterbury.

In this hymn Alford spends one verse directly praising God for the gathering then transfers concern to how the Christian utilises what he has been given. He trusts the follower will not be found wanting and so can look forward with confidence to the day when the Lord returns.

St George's, Windsor

G. J. Elvey 1816-93

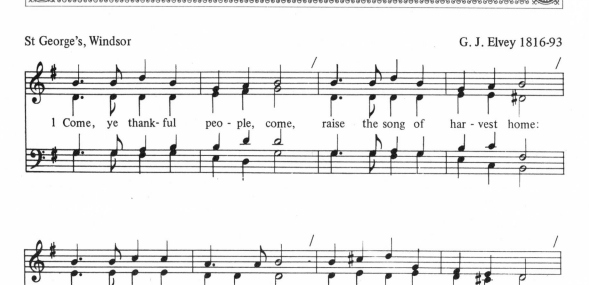

1 Come, ye thank-ful peo-ple, come, raise the song of har-vest home: all is safe-ly gath-er'd in, ere the win-ter storms be-gin;

God our ma-ker doth pro-vide for our wants to be supp-lied:

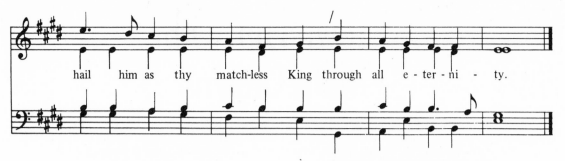

hail him as thy match-less King through all e - ter - ni - ty.

2 Crown him the Lord of life,
who triumphed o'er the grave,
and rose victorious in the strife
for those he came to save;
his glories now we sing
who died, and rose on high,
who died — eternal life to bring,
and lives, that death may die.

3 Crown him the Lord of peace,
whose power a sceptre sways
from pole to pole, that wars may cease,
and all be prayer and praise:
his reign shall know no end,
and round his pierced feet
fair flowers of paradise extend,
their fragrance ever sweet.

4 Crown him the Lord of love;
behold his hands and side,
those wounds, yet visible above,
in beauty glorified:
all hail, Redeemer, hail!
for thou hast died for me:
thy praise and glory shall not fail
throughout eternity.

Matthew Bridges 1800-94;
Godfrey Thring 1823-1903

Day by Day

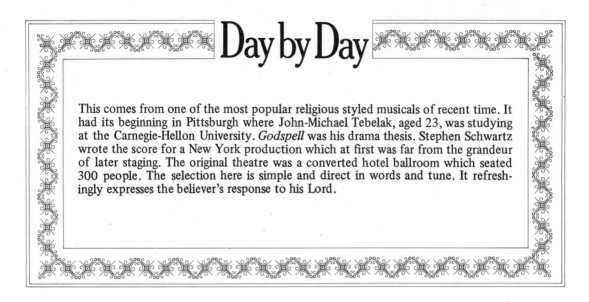

This comes from one of the most popular religious styled musicals of recent time. It had its beginning in Pittsburgh where John-Michael Tebelak, aged 23, was studying at the Carnegie-Hellon University. *Godspell* was his drama thesis. Stephen Schwartz wrote the score for a New York production which at first was far from the grandeur of later staging. The original theatre was a converted hotel ballroom which seated 300 people. The selection here is simple and direct in words and tune. It refreshingly expresses the believer's response to his Lord.

(from the musical production *Godspell*)

Stephen Schwartz

THE SUN THAT BIDS US REST IS WAKING
OUR BRETHREN 'NEATH THE WESTERN SKY,
& HOUR BY HOUR FRESH LIPS ARE MAKING
THY WONDROUS DOINGS HEARD ON HIGH.

"The Day Thou Gavest, Lord, Is Ended" Verse 4

The Day Thou Gavest Lord Is Ended

John Ellerton was a clergyman. This was written in the first instance for *Liturgy For Missionary Meetings* with subsequent revision when included in the 1871 publication *Church Poetry*. The undoubted popularity it now has was first boosted when it was selected by Queen Victoria for her Diamond Jubilee. Several writers have said this hymn personifies the atmosphere of the rural British parish church and also the spirit of the famous hymn book of the Church of England, *Hymns Ancient and Modern*. Ellerton's hymn links all parts of the world together under the rule of day. On this kingdom the sun never sets. There is no darkness.

St Clement

C. C. Scholefield 1839-1904

1 The day thou gav - est, Lord, is end - ed, the dark - ness

falls at thy be - hest; to thee our morn - ing

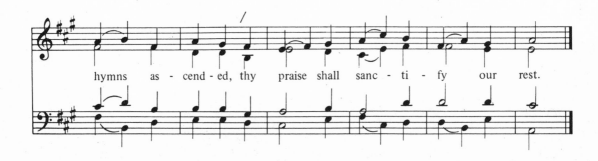

hymns as - cend - ed, thy praise shall sanc - ti - fy our rest.

2 We thank thee that thy Church unsleeping,
while earth rolls onward into light,
through all the world her watch is keeping
and rests not now by day or night.

3 As o'er each continent and island
the dawn leads on another day,
the voice of prayer is never silent,
nor dies the strain of praise away.

4 The sun that bids us rest is waking
our brethren 'neath the western sky,
and hour by hour fresh lips are making
thy wondrous doings heard on high.

5 So be it, Lord; thy throne shall never,
like earth's proud empires, pass away;
thy kingdom stands, and grows for ever,
till all thy creatures own thy sway.

John Ellerton 1826-93

DEAR LORD & FATHER OF MANKIND,
FORGIVE OUR FOOLISH WAYS;
RE-CLOTHE US IN OUR RIGHTFUL
MIND;
IN PURER LIVES THY SERVICE FIND,
IN DEEPER REVERENCE, PRAISE.

"Dear Lord and Father of Mankind" Verse 1

Dear Lord and Father of Mankind

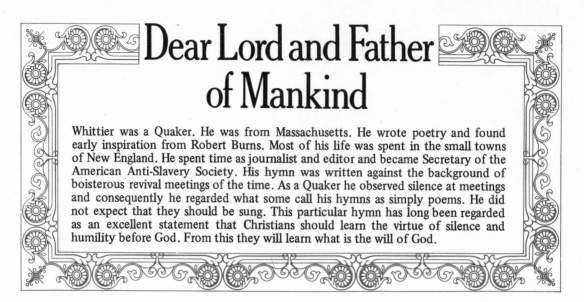

Whittier was a Quaker. He was from Massachusetts. He wrote poetry and found early inspiration from Robert Burns. Most of his life was spent in the small towns of New England. He spent time as journalist and editor and became Secretary of the American Anti-Slavery Society. His hymn was written against the background of boisterous revival meetings of the time. As a Quaker he observed silence at meetings and consequently he regarded what some call his hymns as simply poems. He did not expect that they should be sung. This particular hymn has long been regarded as an excellent statement that Christians should learn the virtue of silence and humility before God. From this they will learn what is the will of God.

Repton

C. H. H. Parry 1848-1918

1 Dear Lord and Fa-ther of man-kind, for-give our fool-ish ways; re-clothe us in our right-ful mind; in pur-er lives thy ser-vice find, in

deep-er re - v'rence, praise, in deep-er re - v'rence, praise.

(The last line of each verse is sung twice)

2 In simple trust like theirs who heard,
   beside the Syrian sea,
   the gracious calling of the Lord,
   let us, like them., without a word
   rise up and follow thee.

3 O Sabbath rest by Galilee!
   O calm of hills above,
   where Jesus knelt to share with thee
   the silence of eternity,
   interpreted by love!

4 With that deep hush subduing all
   our words and works that drown
   the tender whisper of thy call,
   as noiseless let thy blessing fall
   as fell thy manna down.

5 Drop thy still dews of quietness,
   till all our strivings cease;
   take from our souls the strain and stress,
   and let our ordered lives confess
   the beauty of thy peace.

6 Breathe through the heats of our desire
   thy coolness and thy balm;
   let sense be dumb, let flesh retire;
   speak through the earthquake, wind, and fire,
   O still small voice of calm!

John Greenleaf Whittier 1807-92

RINITY OF LOVE & POWER,
OUR BRETHREN SHIELD IN DANGER'S
HOUR ;
FROM ROCK & TEMPEST, FIRE & FOE,
PROTECT THEM WHERESOE'ER
THEY GO;
AND EVER LET THERE RISE TO THEE
GLAD HYMNS OF PRAISE FROM LAND
& SEA.

"Eternal Father, Strong to Save" Verse 4

Eternal Father, Strong to

This hymn was written for the 1861 *Hymns Ancient and Modern* with sligh
sion from its original form of the previous year. The writer was Master at Winch
College Choristers' School in England. At least 12 hymns bear his name but n
have enjoyed the success of this one. It has been particularly popular with sailo
and fishermen. A verse is given to each Person of the Godhead with final direction
toward the threefold God. It is a prayer for those who travel the seas.

Melita

J. B. Dykes 1823-76

1 Eternal Father, strong to save, whose arm doth bind the restless wave, who bidd'st the mighty ocean deep its own appointed limits keep: Oh, hear us when we cry to thee for those in peril on the sea!

2 O Saviour, whose almighty word
   the winds and waves submissive heard,
   who walkedst on the foaming deep,
   and calm amidst its rage didst sleep:
   Oh, hear us when we cry to thee
   for those in peril on the sea!

3 O sacred Spirit, who didst brood
   upon the chaos dark and rude,
   who bad'st its angry tumult cease,
   and gavest light, and life, and peace:
   Oh, hear us when we cry to thee
   for those in peril on the sea!

4 O Trinity of love and power,
   our brethren shield in danger's hour;
   from rock and tempest, fire and foe,
   protect them wheresoe'er they go;
   and ever let there rise to thee
   glad hymns of praise from land and sea.

William Whiting 1825-78

For All the Saints

This was first published in 1864. One imagines the writer was inspired by Hebrews 11 for in his hymn he insists on the same basic underlying Christian quality so well put in that Scripture passage, that of faith. The Vaughan Williams' tune, *Sine Nomine*, elevates this hymn and makes it a fine processional hymn of tribute to Saints down the ages.

Sine Nomine

Ralph Vaughan Williams 1872-1958

1 For all the saints who from their la - bours rest, who

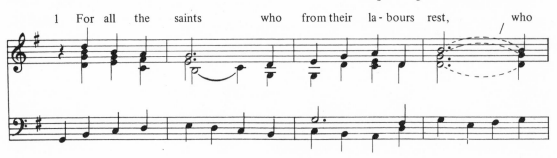

thee by faith be - 'fore the world con - fessed, / thy

name, O Je - sus, be for e - ver blest. **REFRAIN** *Al -*

- le - lu - ia,   al - le - lu - ia!

(The Alleluia Refrain is sung at the end of each verse)

2 Thou wast their rock, their fortress, and their might;
 thou, Lord, their captain in the well-fought fight;
 thou in the darkness drear their one true light.

3 Oh, may thy soldiers, faithful, true and bold,
 fight as the saints who nobly fought of old,
 and win, with them, the victor's crown of gold!

4 O blest communion, fellowship divine!
 we feebly struggle; they in glory shine,
 yet all are one in thee, for all are thine.

5 And when the strife is fierce, the warfare long,
 steals on the ear the distant triumph-song,
 and hearts are brave again, and arms are strong.

6 The golden evening brightens in the west;
 soon, soon to faithful warriors cometh rest;
 sweet is the calm of Paradise the blest.

7 But Lo! there breaks a yet more glorious day:
 the saints triumphant rise in bright array;
 the King of glory passes on his way.

8 From earth's wide bounds, from ocean's farthest coast,
 through gates of pearl streams in the countless host,
 singing to Father, Son, and Holy Ghost.

William Walsham How 1823-97

God of Concrete, God of Steel

The writer is the head of a British theological college and well known in musical circles. When ministering in the city of Sheffield he was aware of how his young people found more traditional hymns dull, sentimental, or inappropriate for their culture. He vowed he would produce something which used the symbols which speak of contemporary life. The result was this hymn with its basic affirmation that God is of all.

New Horizons

arr. F. B. Westbrook 1903-75

1 God of con-crete, God of steel, God of pis-ton and of wheel,

God of py-lon, God of steam, God of gir-der and of beam,

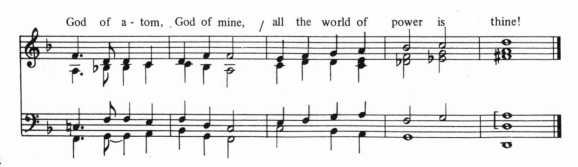

God of a-tom, God of mine, all the world of power is thine!

2 Lord of cable, Lord of rail,
  Lord of motorway and mail,
  Lord of rocket, Lord of flight,
  Lord of soaring satellite,
  Lord of lightning's livid line,
  all the world of speed is thine!

3 Lord of science, Lord of art,
  God of map and graph and chart,
  Lord of physics and research,
  Word of Bible, Faith of Church,
  Lord of sequence and design,
  all the world of truth is thine!

4 God whose glory fills the earth,
  gave the universe its birth,
  loosed the Christ with Easter's might,
  saves the world from evil's blight,
  claims mankind by grace divine,
  all the world of love is thine!

Richard G. Jones 1926—

Guide Me O Thou Great Jehovah

William Williams was known as the sweet singer of Wales. He was a deacon and curate but never took orders. His first book of hymns, *Alleluia,* 1744 ran into three editions and there followed five editions for *Welsh Hymns,* 1762. His English translator Peter Williams was a student at Carmarthen College and apparently warned that he should not hear Whitefield. He did and was converted. Earliest English use of the hymn came through inclusion in the hymn book used by the Sussex Chapels of the Countess of Huntingdon Connexion. The hymn has become popular worldwide but few would argue that the Welsh still sing it best.

Cwm Rhondda

J. Hughes 1873-1932

1 Guide me, O thou great Je - ho - vah, pil - grim through this bar - ren land; I am weak, but thou art might - y; hold me with thy pow'r - ful hand: bread of hea - ven, bread of hea - ven!

feed me now and e - ver - more, feed me now and e - ver - more.

(The last two lines of each verse are each repeated)

2 Open thou the crystal fountain,
  whence the healing stream shall flow;
  let the fiery, cloudy pillar
  lead me all my journey through:
  strong deliverer!
  be thou still my help and shield.

3 When I tread the verge of Jordan,
  bid my anxious fears subside;
  death of deaths, and hell's destruction,
  land me safe on Canaan's side:
  songs of praises
  I will ever give to thee.

William Williams 1717-91
tr. Peter Williams 1722-96

Holy, Holy, Holy, Lord God Almighty!

Bishop Heber was born in Cheshire in England and was termed a model clergyman. He wrote 57 hymns and one critic of his time said he enshrined in his hymns the lyric spirit of Scott and Byron. Tennyson said this was his favourite hymn. It expounds the Doctrine of the Trinity and gives chance and reason for the Christian to praise God, the thrice Holy, Father, Son and Holy Ghost.

Nicea

J. B. Dykes 1823-76

1 Holy, holy, holy, Lord God almighty! Early in the morning our song shall rise to thee; holy, holy, holy, merciful and mighty, God in three persons, blessed Trinity!

2 Holy, holy, holy; all the saints adore thee,
   casting down their golden crowns around the glassy sea;
   cherubim and seraphim falling down before thee,
   who wert, and art, and evermore shalt be.

3 Holy, holy, holy; though the darkness hide thee,
   though the eye of sinful man thy glory may not see,
   only thou art holy; there is none beside thee
   perfect in power, in love, and purity!

4 Holy, holy, holy, Lord God Almighty!
   All thy works shall praise thy name in earth and sky and sea;
   holy, holy, holy, merciful and mighty,
   God in three Persons, blessèd Trinity!

Reginald Heber 1783-1826

How Great Thou Art

The popularity of this hymn owes much to the worldwide ministry of Dr Billy Graham. It was sung with power by his campaign soloist George Beverly Shea. It is regularly heard at the commencement of the Graham organisation's The Hour of Decision, its radio ministry programme which has a global listening audience. The verse tells of God's mighty works. The chorus with its sudden uplift in tune speaks with power of the only response which can be made in the face of such 'works' and this is to say 'How Great Thou Art'.

O Store Gud

Swedish traditional melody

1 O Lord my God! when I in awe-some won-der con-si-der all the works thy hand hath made, I see the stars, I hear the might-y thun-der, thy pow'r through-out the un-i-verse dis-play'd:

REFRAIN

then sings my soul, my Sa-viour God, to

thee, how great thou art! how great thou art! Then sings my soul, my Sa-viour God, to

thee, how great thou art! how great thou art!

ALTERNATIVE ENDING

thee, how great thou art! how great thou art!

(The refrain is sung after each verse)

2 When through the woods and forest glades I wander
and hear the birds sing sweetly in the trees:
when I look down from lofty mountain grandeur,
and hear the brook, and feel the gentle breeze:

3 And when I think: that God, his Son not sparing,
sent him to die – I scarce can take it in:
that on the cross, my burden gladly bearing,
he bled and died, to take away my sin:

4 When Christ shall come with shout of acclamation
and take me home – what joy shall fill my heart!
Then shall I bow, in humble adoration,
and there proclaim: My God, how great thou art!

English words © 1953 by Stuart K. Hine 1899–

Optional extra verses:

3a Oh, when I see ungrateful man defiling
this bounteous earth, God's gifts so good and great;
in foolish pride, God's holy name reviling
and yet, in grace, his wrath and judgement wait:

3b When burdens press, and seem beyond endurance,
bowed down with grief, to him I lift my face;
and then in love he brings me sweet assurance:
'My child! for thee sufficient is my grace.'

© 1958 Stuart K. Hine

61

How Sweet the Name

In the 1779 *Olney Hymns* this was titled *The Name of Jesus*. John Wesley chose it for inclusion in the *Arminian Magazine*, 1781. John Newton was ordained Curate of the market town of Olney in Buckinghamshire, England, in 1764. With William Cowper he composed numerous hymns. Newton preached beyond his eightieth birthday. It was said that a servant traced the text lines with a pointer.

The theme is plain. It is of Jesus's name and here the power and force of this name is given flesh.

St Peter

A. R. Reinagle 1799-1877

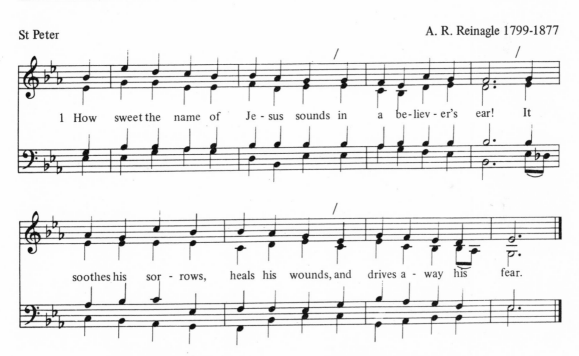

1 How sweet the name of Je - sus sounds in a be - liev - er's ear! It soothes his sor - rows, heals his wounds, and drives a - way his fear.

2 It makes the wounded spirit whole,
and calms the troubled breast;
'tis manna to the hungry soul,
and to the weary rest.

3 Dear name! the rock on which I build,
my shield, and hiding-place,
my never-failing treasury, filled
with boundless stores of grace!

4 Jesus, my shepherd, brother, friend,
my prophet, priest, and king,
my Lord, my life, my way, my end,
accept the praise I bring.

5 Weak is the effort of my heart,
and cold my warmest thought;
but when I see thee as thou art
I'll praise thee as I ought.

6 Till then I would thy love proclaim
with every fleeting breath;
and may the music of thy name
refresh my soul in death.

John Newton 1725-1807

I Need Thee Every Hour

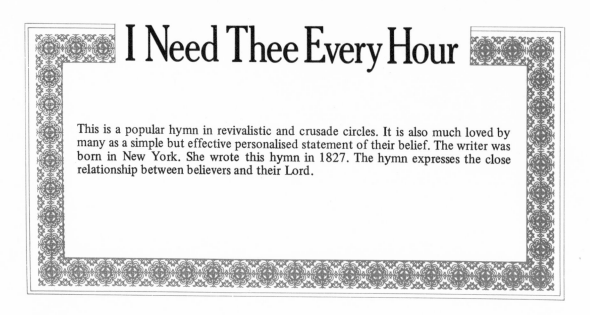

This is a popular hymn in revivalistic and crusade circles. It is also much loved by many as a simple but effective personalised statement of their belief. The writer was born in New York. She wrote this hymn in 1827. The hymn expresses the close relationship between believers and their Lord.

I Need Thee

R. Lowry 1826-99

1 I need thee eve-ry hour, most gra - cious Lord; no ten - der voice like thine can peace af - ford.

REFRAIN

I need thee, oh, I need thee, eve - ry hour I need thee; oh,

bless   me   now, my   Sa - viour; I   come   to   thee.

(The refrain is sung after each verse)

2 I need thee every hour;
   stay thou near by:
   temptations lose their power
   when thou art nigh.

3 I need thee every hour,
   in joy or pain;
   come quickly and abide,
   or life is vain.

4 I need thee every hour;
   teach me thy will,
   and thy rich promises
   in me fulfil.

Annie Sherwood Hawks
1835-1918

In the Name of Jesus

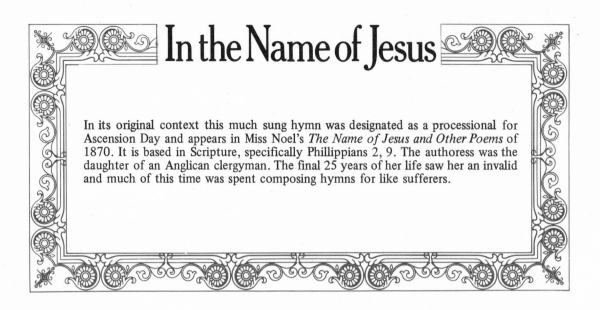

In its original context this much sung hymn was designated as a processional for Ascension Day and appears in Miss Noel's *The Name of Jesus and Other Poems* of 1870. It is based in Scripture, specifically Phillippians 2, 9. The authoress was the daughter of an Anglican clergyman. The final 25 years of her life saw her an invalid and much of this time was spent composing hymns for like sufferers.

Evelyns

W. H. Monk 1823-89

1 In the name of Je - sus eve - ry knee shall bow, eve - ry tongue con - fess him King of glo - ry now. 'Tis the Fa - ther's plea - sure we should call him Lord, who from the be - gin - ning was the might - y Word.

2 Humbled for a season,
   to receive a name
   from the lips of sinners
   unto whom he came,
   faithfully he bore it
   spotless to the last,
   brought it back victorious
   when from death he passed.

3 Name him, brothers, name him,
   with love as strong as death,
   but with awe and wonder,
   and with bated breath;
   he is God the Saviour,
   he is Christ the Lord,
   ever to be worshipped,
   trusted, and adored.

4 In your hearts enthrone him;
   there let him subdue
   all that is not holy,
   all that is not true;
   crown him as your captain
   in temptation's hour;
   let his will enfold you
   in its light and power.

5 Brothers, this Lord Jesus
   shall return again
   with his Father's glory,
   with his angel train;
   for all wreaths of empire
   meet upon his brow,
   and our hearts confess him
   King of glory now.

Caroline Maria Noel
1817-77

Jesus Lives Thy Terrors Now

This is based on John 14, 19. The use of 'Hallelujah' is not found in the original source. Christian Gellert is one of the most famous and respected German hymnologists. He was born in Saxony and in later life he was a professor at Leipzig University where once he was a theological student.

This hymn speaks good news for those who fear death. It tells of death's defeat by Jesus. In its fourth verse it captures something of the splendid triumph found in the last verses of Romans 8.

St Albinus

H. J. Gauntlett 1805-76

1 Jesus lives! thy terrors now
can, O death, no more appal us;
Jesus lives! by this we know
thou, O grave, canst not enthral us. Hallelujah!

(The Hallelujah is sung at the end of each verse)

2 Jesus lives! to him the throne
high o'er heaven and earth is given;
we may go where he is gone,
live and reign with him in heaven.

3 Jesus lives! for us he died;
hence may we, to Jesus living,
pure in heart and act abide,
praise to him and glory giving.

4 Jesus lives! our hearts know well
nought from us his love shall sever;
life, nor death, nor powers of hell,
part us now from Christ for ever.

5 Jesus lives! henceforth is death
entrance-gate of life immortal;
this shall calm our trembling breath
when we pass its gloomy portal.

Christian Fürchtegott Gellert   *tr.* Frances Elizabeth Cox 1812-97

ВОСКРЕСЕНИЕ ГДА И БГА И СПА НАШЕГШ ІИСА ХРТА

Jesu, Lover of My Soul

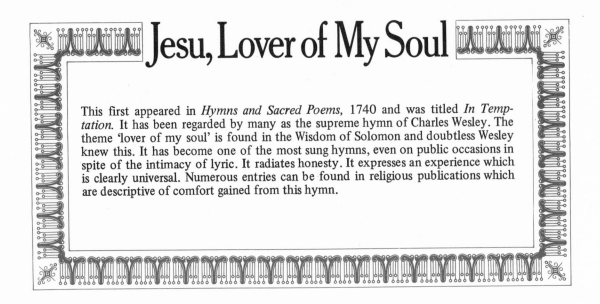

This first appeared in *Hymns and Sacred Poems,* 1740 and was titled *In Temptation.* It has been regarded by many as the supreme hymn of Charles Wesley. The theme 'lover of my soul' is found in the Wisdom of Solomon and doubtless Wesley knew this. It has become one of the most sung hymns, even on public occasions in spite of the intimacy of lyric. It radiates honesty. It expresses an experience which is clearly universal. Numerous entries can be found in religious publications which are descriptive of comfort gained from this hymn.

Hollingside

J. B. Dykes 1823-76

1 Je - su, lo - ver of my soul, let me to thy bo - som fly,

while the near - er wa - ters roll, while the tem - pest still is high:

hide me, O my Sa - viour, hide, till the storm of life be past;

safe in-to the ha-ven guide, oh, re-ceive my soul at last.

2 Other refuge have I none,
hangs my helpless soul on thee;
leave, ah! leave me not alone,
still support and comfort me:
all my trust on thee is stayed,
all my help from thee I bring;
cover my defenceless head
with the shadow of thy wing.

3 Thou, O Christ, art all I want,
more than all in thee I find.
Raise the fallen, cheer the faint,
heal the sick, and lead the blind:
just and holy is thy name,
I am all unrighteousness;
false and full of sin I am,
thou art full of truth and grace.

4 Plenteous grace with thee is found,
grace to cover all my sin;
let the healing streams abound,
make and keep me pure within:
thou of life the fountain art,
freely let me take of thee,
spring thou up within my heart,
rise to all eternity.

Charles Wesley 1707-88

Jesus the Lord, Said

This song was translated from the Urdu by Dermott Monahan. It has quickly become a favourite of young people with gradual acceptance from those older. It expresses four claims made by Jesus as stated in the fourth Gospel. When sung each verse is treated in similar fashion to the full version given of the first.

Urdu melody
arr. F. B. Westbrook 1903-75

Yisu ne kaha

1 Je - sus the Lord said: 'I am the Bread, the Bread of Life for man - kind am I. The

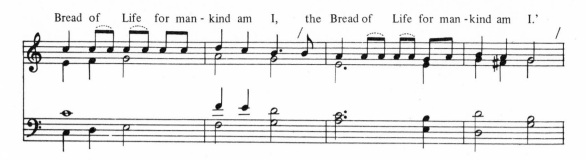

Bread of Life for man-kind am I, the Bread of Life for man-kind am I.'

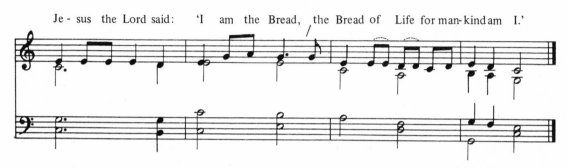

Je-sus the Lord said: 'I am the Bread, the Bread of Life for man-kind am I.'

2 Jesus the Lord said: 'I am the Door,
   the Way and the Door for the poor am I.' etc.

3 Jesus the Lord said: 'I am the Light,
   the one true Light of the world am I.' etc.

4 Jesus the Lòrd said: 'I am the Shepherd,
   the one Good Shepherd of the sheep am I.' etc.

5 Jesus the Lord said: 'I am the Life,
   the Resurrection and the Life am I.' etc.

Anonymous Urdu
tr. Dermott Monahan 1906-57

Kum Ba Yah

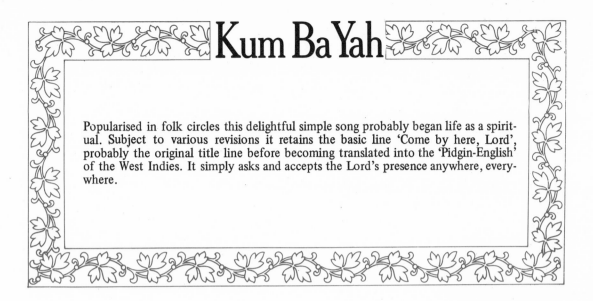

Popularised in folk circles this delightful simple song probably began life as a spiritual. Subject to various revisions it retains the basic line 'Come by here, Lord', probably the original title line before becoming translated into the 'Pidgin-English' of the West Indies. It simply asks and accepts the Lord's presence anywhere, everywhere.

Traditional Caribbean
arr. Colin Mayheather 1952—

2 Someone's crying, Lord, kumbayah. . . .

3 Someone's singing, Lord, kumbayah. . . .

4 Someone's praying, Lord, kumbayah. . . .

(Other verses may be made up by the singers) Traditional Spiritual

Lead, Kindly Light

This was written in 1833 and published the following year in the *British Magazine* under the title of *Faith in Heavenly Leadings.* In other sources the title was *Unto the Godly There Ariseth Up Light in the Darkness.* Newman wrote his hymn when he felt personal death was near. It became particularly popular during the Welsh Revival of 1905. Vivid in imagery, especially so for those familiar with rural living, the hymn talks the language of pilgrimage, guidance and perseverance.

Sandon

C. H. Purday 1799-1885

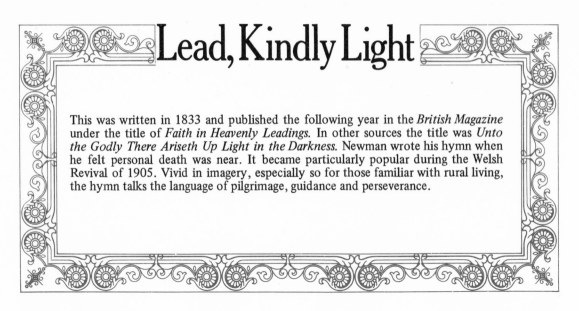

1 Lead, kind-ly Light, a - mid th'en-cir-cling gloom lead thou me on!

The night is dark, and I am far from home; lead thou me on! Keep thou my

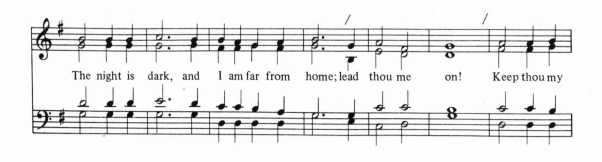

feet; I do not ask to see the dis-tant scene: one step e-nough for me.

2 I was not ever thus, nor prayed that thou
  shouldst lead me on.
  I loved to choose and see my path, but now
  lead thou me on!
  I loved the garish day, and, spite of fears,
  pride ruled my will: remember not past years.

3 So long thy power hath blest me, sure it still
  will lead me on
  o'er moor and fen, o'er crag and torrent, till
  the night is gone;
  and with the morn those angel faces smile
  which I have loved long since, and lost awhile.

John Henry Newman 1801-90

Let Us Break Bread Together

This Negro spiritual is the essence of simplicity both in words and tune. It first found use amongst young people for it lends itself to acoustic guitar accompaniment and a loose framework of worship. Gradually it has become a favourite of all ages. Its acceptance amongst older Christians was clearly shown by its inclusion on a late 1970s album *The Old Rugged Cross* by long-standing and revered gospel singer George Beverly Shea. The song is often used at the communion service. Its message reminds Christians of their spiritual food and drink.

Negro Spiritual
arr. Colin Mayheather 1952—

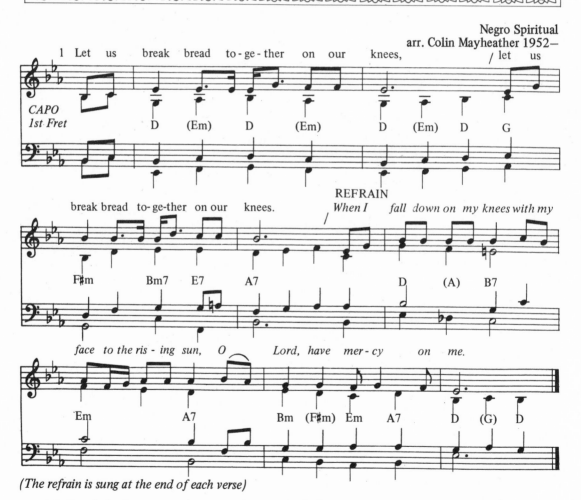

(The refrain is sung at the end of each verse)

2 Let us drink wine together on our knees,
   let us drink wine together on our knees.

3 Let us praise God together on our knees,
   let us praise God together on our knees.

Traditional Spiritual

78

DANCE, THEN, WHEREVER YOU MAY
BE;
I AM THE LORD OF THE DANCE, SAID
HE;
& I'LL LEAD YOU ALL WHEREVER
YOU MAY BE,
& I'LL LEAD YOU ALL IN THE DANCE,
SAID HE.

"Lord of the Dance" Refrain

Lord of the Dance

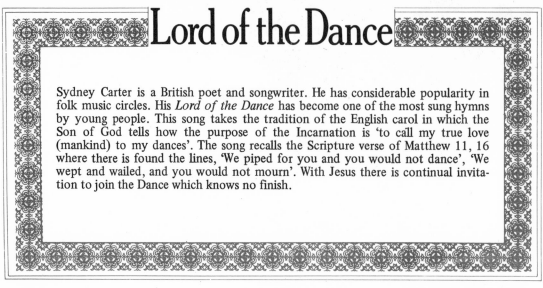

Sydney Carter is a British poet and songwriter. He has considerable popularity in folk music circles. His *Lord of the Dance* has become one of the most sung hymns by young people. This song takes the tradition of the English carol in which the Son of God tells how the purpose of the Incarnation is 'to call my true love (mankind) to my dances'. The song recalls the Scripture verse of Matthew 11, 16 where there is found the lines, 'We piped for you and you would not dance', 'We wept and wailed, and you would not mourn'. With Jesus there is continual invitation to join the Dance which knows no finish.

Adapted from a Shaker melody by Sydney Carter 1915—
arr. A. E. Mathew

Lord of the Dance

I danced in the morn-ing when the world was be-gun, and I danced in the moon and the stars and the sun; amd I came down from hea-ven and I danced on the earth, at Beth-le-hem I had my birth.

Dance, then, wher-e-ver you may be; I am the Lord of the Dance, said he; and I'll lead you all wher-e-ver you may be, and I'll lead you all in the Dance, said he.

(The refrain is sung after each verse)

2 I danced for the scribe and the pharisee,
   but they would not dance and they wouldn't follow me.
   I danced for the fishermen, for James and John —
   they came with me and the dance went on:

3 I danced on the Sabbath and I cured the lame;
   the holy people said it was a shame.
   They whipped and they stripped and they hung me on high;
   and they left me there on a cross to die.

4 I danced on a Friday when the sky turned black;
   it's hard to dance with the devil on your back.
   They buried my body and they thought I'd gone;
   but I am the dance and I still go on:

5 They cut me down and I leap up high,
   I am the life that'll never, never die;
   I'll live in you if you'll live in me;
   I am the Lord of the Dance, said he:

Sydney Carter 1915—

THE LORD'S MY SHEPHERD, I'LL NOT WANT;
HE MAKES ME DOWN TO LIE
IN PASTURES GREEN; HE LEADETH ME
THE QUIET WATERS BY.

"The Lord's My Shepherd" Verse 1

AND IN GOD'S
HOUSE FOR EVERMORE

MY DWELLING
PLACE SHALL BE

The Lord's My Shepherd

William Whittingham's *The Lord is Only My Support* was published in 1556. From this Francis Rous composed his version. Whittingham married John Calvin's sister and succeeded John Knox as Pastor of the English Church in Geneva, Switzerland. Rous studied law. He became Minister of Parliament for Truro, Cornwall, in the British Parliament, was Provost of Eton, and a member of Cromwell's Privy Council.

The hymn has been particularly dear to Scottish peoples. It was chosen by Queen Elizabeth II for her marriage service. The source is from Scripture, Psalm 23.

Crimond

J. S. Irvine 1836-87

1 The Lord's my shep - herd, I'll not want; he makes me down to lie in pas - tures green; he lead - eth me the qui - et wa - ters by.

2 My soul he doth restore again,
   and me to walk doth make
   within the paths of righteousness
   e'en for his own name's sake.

3 Yea, though I walk in death's dark vale,
   yet will I fear no ill;
   for thou art with me, and thy rod
   and staff me comfort still.

4 My table thou has furnishèd
   in presence of my foes;
   my head thou dost with oil anoint,
   and my cup overflows.

5 Goodness and mercy all my life
   shall surely follow me,
   and in God's house for evermore
   my dwelling-place shall be.

Scottish Psalter 1650

The Lord's Prayer

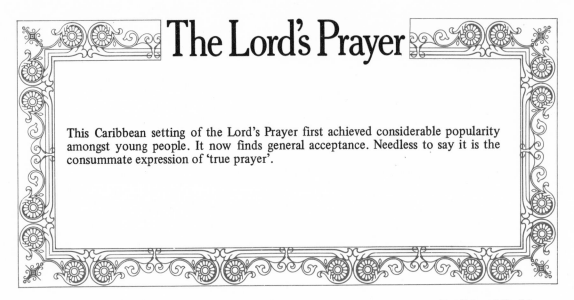

This Caribbean setting of the Lord's Prayer first achieved considerable popularity amongst young people. It now finds general acceptance. Needless to say it is the consummate expression of 'true prayer'.

Traditional Caribbean
arr. Colin Mayheather 1952—

1 Our Fa-ther, who art in hea-ven,

hal-low-ed be thy name! Thy king-dom come, thy

will be done, *hal-low-ed be thy* name! name!

(The Refrain hallowèd be thy name! *is sung after each line)*

2 On the earth as it is in heaven.
   Give us this day our daily bread.

3 Forgive us all our trespasses,
   as we forgive those who trespass against us.

4 And lead us not into temptation,
   but deliver us from all that is evil.

5 For thine is the kingdom, the power, and the glory
   for ever and for ever and ever.

6 Amen, Amen, it shall be so,
   Amen, Amen, it shall be so.

Traditional Caribbean

Love Divine All Loves Excelling

A famous hymn of Charles Wesley's. It burns with passion and conviction. It builds steadily toward the final crescendo of the last two lines. Wesley's hymns are always marked by liveliness and urgency. His belief was sure.

R. H. Prichard 1811-87
arr. Peter Faber 1947—

Hyfrydol

1 Love di - vine, all loves ex - cel - ling, joy of heav'n to earth come down; fix in us thy humb - le dwel - ling, all thy faith - ful mer - cies crown: Je - sus,

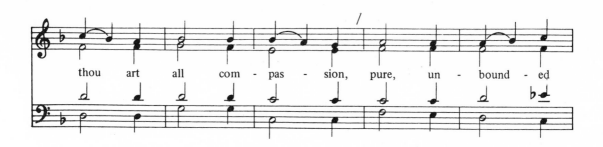

thou art all com - pas - sion, pure, un - bound - ed

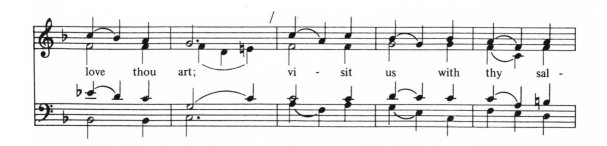

love thou art; vi - sit us with thy sal -

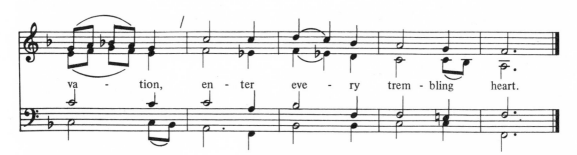

va - tion, en - ter eve - ry trem - bling heart.

2 Come, almighty, to deliver,
let us all thy grace receive:
suddenly return, and never,
never more thy temples leave:
thee we would be always blessing,
serve thee as thy hosts above,
pray, and praise thee, without ceasing,
glory in thy perfect love.

3 Finish then thy new creation,
pure and spotless let us be;
let us see thy great salvation,
perfectly restored in thee;
changed from glory into glory,
till in heaven we take our place,
till we cast our crowns before thee,
lost in wonder, love, and praise.

Charles Wesley 1707-88

Man of Sorrows

Writer Philip Bliss is familiar for other hymns of more overtly revivalistic nature such as *Whosoever Heareth* and *Brightly Beams Our Father's Mercy.* This hymn is more restrained with a simple refrain as climax to each statement made concerning the Cross and its meaning. Bliss was born in the Pennsylvania town of Clearfield in 1838.

Gethsemane

P. Bliss 1838-76

1 Man of sor - rows! what a name for the Son of God, who came ru - in'd sin - ners to re - claim! Hal - le - lu - jah! what a Sa - viour!

(The refrain is sung at the end of each verse)

2 Bearing shame and scoffing rude,
in my place condemned he stood;
sealed my pardon with his blood:

3 Guilty, vile, and helpless we;
spotless Lamb of God was he:
full atonement — can it be?

4 Lifted up was he to die.
It is finished! was his cry;
now in heaven exalted high:

5 When he comes, our glorious King,
all his ransomed home to bring,
then anew this song we'll sing:

Philip Bliss 1838-76

Mine Eyes Have Seen

Mrs Howe was born in New York. She was known as a passionate abolitionist and supporter of social causes. The hymn with tune here given has become known as *The Battle Hymn of the Republic* which derives from a title given to Mrs Howe's verses when published in the magazine *Atlantic Monthly* of February 1862.

The hymn speaks clearly of the ever-growing Kingdom with consequent call upon each and every one to further its progress.

Battle Hymn

Adapted from American Camp Meeting Song 1861

1 Mine eyes have seen the glo-ry of the com-ing of the Lord: he is tramp-ling out the vin - tage where the grapes of wrath are stored; he hath loos'd the fate-ful light-ning of his ter - ri - ble swift sword: his truth is march-ing on.

Glory, glory, halle-lu - jah, glory, glory halle-lu - jah,

glory, glory, halle-lu - jah, his truth is march-ing on.

(The refrain is sung after each verse)

2 He hath sounded forth the trumpet that shall never call retreat;
he is sifting out the hearts of men before his judgement-seat:
oh, be swift, my soul, to answer him; be jubilant, my feet!
Our God is marching on.

3 In the beauty of the lilies Christ was born across the sea,
with a glory in his bosom that transfigures you and me:
as he died to make men holy, let us live to make men free,
while God is marching on.

Julia Ward Howe 1819-1910

Morning Has Broken

Author and poet Eleanor Farjeon was born in London. Her father was also a writer. Eleanor Farjeon is known for her children's books and in 1956 she won the Carnegie Medal for her book *The Little Bookroom. Morning Has Broken* has become one of the best known hymns outside immediate Christian circles. It has achieved this in slightly unusual fashion. A British born singer-songwriter Cat Stevens sang it into the hit-parades of numerous countries during 1972. The words express refreshing innocence and a child-like appreciation and wonder in which the senses are all important.

Bunessan

Gaelic melody
harmonized by Martin Shaw 1875-1958

1 Morn-ing has bro-ken like the first morn-ing; black-bird has spo-ken like the first bird.

Praise for the sing-ing, praise for the morn-ing, praise for them, spring-ing fresh from the word.

2 Sweet the rain's new fall
sunlit from heaven,
like the first dewfall
on the first grass.
Praise for the sweetness
of the wet garden,
sprung from completeness
where his feet pass.

3 Mine is the sunlight;
mine is the morning
born of the one light
Eden saw play.
Praise with elation,
praise every morning,
God's re-creation
of the new day.

Eleanor Farjeon 1881-1965

My Song Is Love Unknown

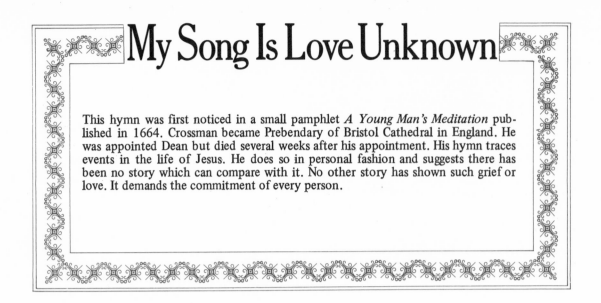

This hymn was first noticed in a small pamphlet *A Young Man's Meditation* published in 1664. Crossman became Prebendary of Bristol Cathedral in England. He was appointed Dean but died several weeks after his appointment. His hymn traces events in the life of Jesus. He does so in personal fashion and suggests there has been no story which can compare with it. No other story has shown such grief or love. It demands the commitment of every person.

Love Unknown   J. N. Ireland 1879-1962

1 My song is love un-known; my Sa-viour's love to me; love to the love-less shown, that they might love-ly be. Oh, who am I, that for my sake, my Lord should take frail flesh and die.

2 He came from his blest throne,
  salvation to bestow;
  but men made strange, and none
  the longed-for Christ would know.
  But O my friend!
  my friend indeed,
  who at my need
  his life did spend.

3 Sometimes they strew his way,
  and his sweet praises sing;
  resounding all the day,
  Hosannas to their King.
  Then: Crucify!
  is all their breath,
  and for his death
  they thirst and cry.

4 Why, what hath my Lord done?
  What makes this rage and spite?
  He made the lame to run,
  he gave the blind their sight.
  Sweet injuries!
  Yet they at these
  themselves displease
  and 'gainst him rise.

5 They rise and needs will have
  my dear Lord made away;
  a murderer they save;
  the prince of life they slay.
  Yet cheerful he
  to suffering goes,
  that he his foes
  from thence might free.

6 In life, no house, no home
  my Lord on earth might have;
  in death, no friendly tomb
  but what a stranger gave.
  What may I say?
  Heav'n was his home;
  but mine the tomb
  wherein he lay.

7 Here might I stay and sing,
  no story so divine;
  never was love, dear King,
  never was grief like thine.
  This is my friend,
  in whose sweet praise
  I all my days
  could gladly spend.

Samuel Crossman 1624-83

O MAY THIS BOUNTEOUS GOD
THROUGH ALL OUR LIFE BE NEAR US,
WITH EVER-JOYFUL HEARTS
& BLESSÈD PEACE TO CHEER US,
& KEEP US IN HIS GRACE,
& GUIDE US WHEN PERPLEXED,
& FREE US FROM ALL ILLS
IN THIS WORLD & THE NEXT.

"Now Thank We All Our God" Verse 2

Now Thank We All Our God

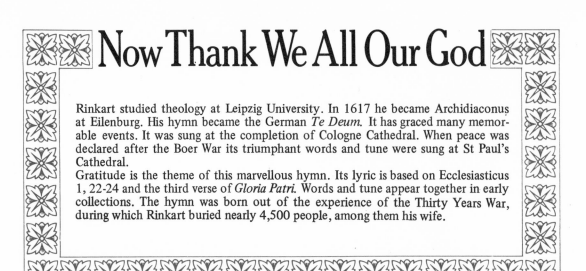

Rinkart studied theology at Leipzig University. In 1617 he became Archidiaconus at Eilenburg. His hymn became the German *Te Deum*. It has graced many memorable events. It was sung at the completion of Cologne Cathedral. When peace was declared after the Boer War its triumphant words and tune were sung at St Paul's Cathedral.

Gratitude is the theme of this marvellous hymn. Its lyric is based on Ecclesiasticus 1, 22-24 and the third verse of *Gloria Patri*. Words and tune appear together in early collections. The hymn was born out of the experience of the Thirty Years War, during which Rinkart buried nearly 4,500 people, among them his wife.

Nun Danket

J. Crüger 1598-1662

1 Now thank we all our God, with hearts, and hands, and voi - ces; who won-drous things hath done, in whom his world re - joi - ces; who, from our mo - thers' arms, hath blessed us on our way with

count-less gifts of love, and still is ours to - day.

2 Oh, may this bounteous God
through all our life be near us,
with ever-joyful hearts
and blessèd peace to cheer us,
and keep us in his grace,
and guide us when perplexed,
and free us from all ills
in this world and the next.

3 All praise and thanks to God
the Father now be given,
the Son, and him who reigns
with them in highest heaven:
the one eternal God,
whom earth and heaven adore;
for thus it was, is now,
and shall be evermore.

Martin Rinkart 1586-1649
tr. Catherine Winkworth 1827-78

Now the day is over,
night is drawing nigh,
shadows of the evening
steal across the sky.

Now the darkness gathers,
stars their watches keep,
birds & beasts & flowers
soon will be asleep.

"Now the Day Is Over" Verses 1 & 2

Now the Day Is Over

This appeared in the British *Church Times,* 1865 and the appendix of *Hymns Ancient and Modern,* 1868. It was written as an evening hymn for scholars at Horbury Bridge, Yorkshire in England. The original second line of verse two was 'Stars begin to peep'. Its base is found in Proverbs 3, 2ff. It asks for safe-keeping and rest for those in need and lest anyone should excuse themselves, its penultimate verse centres on the one thing common to all peoples, death. The last verse puts life in the perspective of the Trinity.

Eudoxia

S. Baring-Gould 1834-1924

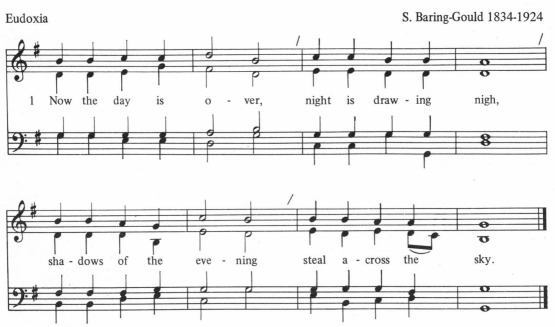

1 Now the day is o - ver, night is draw - ing nigh,
sha - dows of the eve - ning steal a - cross the sky.

2 Now the darkness gathers,
stars their watches keep,
birds and beasts and flowers
soon will be asleep.

3 Jesus, give the weary
calm and sweet repose;
with thy tenderest blessing
may their eyelids close.

4 Grant to little children
visions bright of thee;
guard the sailors tossing
on the angry sea.

5 Comfort every sufferer
watching late in pain;
those who plan some evil
from their sin restrain.

6 Throught the long night-watches
may thine angels spread
their white wings above me,
watching round my bed.

7 When the morning wakens,
then may I arise
pure and fresh and sinless,
in thy holy eyes.

8 Glory to the Father,
glory to the Son,
and to thee, blest Spirit,
whilst all ages run.

Sabine Baring-Gould
1834-1924

O Come All Ye Faithful

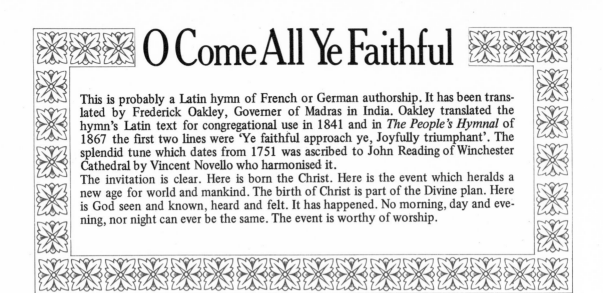

This is probably a Latin hymn of French or German authorship. It has been translated by Frederick Oakley, Governer of Madras in India. Oakley translated the hymn's Latin text for congregational use in 1841 and in *The People's Hymnal* of 1867 the first two lines were 'Ye faithful approach ye, Joyfully triumphant'. The splendid tune which dates from 1751 was ascribed to John Reading of Winchester Cathedral by Vincent Novello who harmonised it.

The invitation is clear. Here is born the Christ. Here is the event which heralds a new age for world and mankind. The birth of Christ is part of the Divine plan. Here is God seen and known, heard and felt. It has happened. No morning, day and evening, nor night can ever be the same. The event is worthy of worship.

Adeste Fideles

J. F. Wade 1711-86

1 O come all ye faith-ful, joy-ful and tri-umph-ant, O come ye, O come ye to Beth-le-hem; come and be-hold him born the King of an-gels: *O come, let us a-dore him, O come let us a-*

REFRAIN

dore him, O come, let us a - dore him, Christ the Lord.

(The refrain is sung after each verse)

2 True God of true God,
   light of light eternal,
   lo, he abhors not the virgin's womb,
   Son of the Father,
   begotten, not created:

3 Sing, choirs of angels,
   sing in exultation,
   sing, all ye citizens of heaven above:
   Glory to God
   in the highest:

4 Yea, Lord, we greet thee,
   born this happy morning;
   Jesu, to thee be glory given,
   Word of the Father,
   now in flesh appearing:

Anon, *tr.* Frederick Oakley
1802-80

O For a Thousand Tongues to Sing

This was originally 18 verses. It stands as perhaps the best known hymn in universal Methodism. Wesley was born at Epworth and died in Marylebone, London. When this hymn received first publication in 1740 it came beneath the heading 'For the Anniversary Day of One's Conversion'. It speaks of the joy of new life in Christ and gives reason why. Several tunes have accompanied this hymn including 'Lydia' and 'Lyngham'.

Richmond

T. Haweis 1734-1820

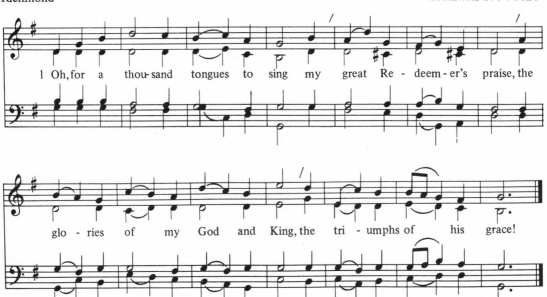

1 Oh, for a thou-sand tongues to sing my great Re-deem-er's praise, the glo - ries of my God and King, the tri - umphs of his grace!

2 My gracious master and my God,
assist me to proclaim,
to spread through all the earth abroad
the honours of thy name.

3 Jesus! the name that charms our fears,
that bids our sorrows cease;
'tis music in the sinner's ears,
'tis life, and health, and peace.

4 He speaks, and, listening to his voice,
new life the dead receive,
the mournful, broken hearts rejoice,
the humble poor believe.

5 He breaks the power of cancelled sin,
he sets the prisoner free;
his blood can make the foulest clean,
his blood availed for me.

6 See all your sins on Jesus laid:
the Lamb of God was slain,
his soul was once an offering made
for every soul of man.

Charles Wesley 1707-88

O God, Our Help in Ages Past

This is based on Psalm 90, 1-5. Renowned hymnologist Dr Erik Routley has called it the 'gravest and most universal of English hymns'. In many hymn books the first line reads, 'Our God, our help in ages past'. It first appeared in Wesley's *Psalms and Hymns,* 1738. It was sung at the funeral of William Gladstone and often features in hymns selected for national and state occasions. Dr Routley says few who heard will forget the impact of its last verse sung in low key by the BBC singers during a short service broadcast in the early morning of 3 September 1939, the day on which the Second World War was declared. The hymn's theme is time. The message is one of comfort.

St Anne

W. Croft 1678-1727

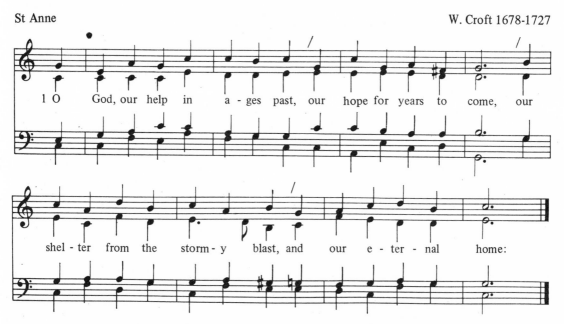

1 O God, our help in a-ges past, our hope for years to come, our shel-ter from the storm-y blast, and our e-ter-nal home:

2 Under the shadow of thy throne,
thy saints have dwelt secure;
sufficient is thine arm alone,
and our defence is sure.

3 Before the hills in order stood,
or earth received her frame,
from everlasting thou art God,
to endless years the same.

4 A thousand ages in thy sight
are like an evening gone;
short as the watch that ends the night
before the rising sun.

5 The busy tribes of flesh and blood,
with all their cares and fears,
are carried downward by the flood,
and lost in following years.

6 Time, like an ever-rolling stream,
bears all its sons away;
they fly forgotten, as a dream
dies at the opening day.

7 O God, our help in ages past,
our hope for years to come,
be thou our guard while troubles last,
and our eternal home.

Isaac Watts 1674-1748

Oh Freedom

This is a popular Negro spiritual and in more recent times much associated with the search of black people for freedom in America. It has been included in several albums recorded by American folk singers of the 1960s. With Freedom as yet a dream for many peoples across the world the song still speaks.

Negro Spiritual
arr. P. Abels

Oh Freedom

(The refrain is sung after each verse)

2 No more moaning, no more moaning,
no more moaning over me!

3 There'll be singing, there'll be singing,
there'll be singing over me!

4 There'll be shouting, there'll be shouting,
there'll be shouting over me!

5 There'll be praying, there'll be praying,
there'll be praying over me!

Traditional Negro Spiritual

"Let us address de Almighty wid pra'r."

On a Hill Far Away

Hymn pollsters often claim this as America's favourite hymn. Its popularity is however worldwide. Its inspiration came from a revival campaign conducted by minister George Bennard in Albion, Michigan, USA. Its message is direct and its lyric is no nonsense evangelical theology. For the believer the crucifixion is very precious.

The Old Rugged Cross

G. Bennard 1873-1958

1 On a hill far a-way stood an old rug-ged cross, the em-blem of suff'ring and shame; and I love that old cross where the dear-est and best for the world of lost sin-ners was slain. *So I'll*

REFRAIN

cher-ish the old rug-ged cross till my

cher-ish the cross, the old rug-ged cross till my tro-phies at last I lay down; I will

cling to the old rug-ged cross and ex-

cling to the cross, the old rug-ged cross and ex-change it some day for a crown.

(The refrain is sung after each verse)

2 Oh, that old rugged cross, so despised by the world,
  has a wondrous attraction for me;
    for the dear Lamb of God left his glory above
    to bear it to dark Calvary.

3 In the old rugged cross, stained with blood so divine,
  a wondrous beauty I see,
    for 'twas on that old cross Jesus suffered and died
    to pardon and sanctify me.

4 To the old rugged cross I will ever be true,
  its shame and reproach gladly bear;
    then he'll call me some day to my home far away,
    where his glory for ever I'll share.

George Bennard 1873-1958

Onward Christian Soldiers

This processional, marching hymn was written for a Sunday-school treat. It was printed in England in the *Church Times* of 1865. Gould was born in Exeter, Devon and was a clergyman. It has been said that Sullivan was surprised his 'brassy', 'martial' tune would prove so popular. There is no mystery in this lyric. The Christian is a member of a victorious army. This army is the Church of God. The hymn suggests a Church perpetually making conquest. There is purpose and movement in the Church of Christ.

St Gertrude

A. Sullivan 1842-1900

1 On-ward! Chris-tian sol-diers, march-ing as to war, with the cross of Je - sus go-ing on be-fore. Christ, the roy-al mas-ter, leads a-gainst the foe; for-ward in-to bat - tle, see! his ban-ners go.

On - ward! Chris - tian sol - diers, march - ing as to war, with the cross of Je - sus go - ing on be - fore.

(The refrain is sung after each verse)

2 At the sign of triumph
Satan's host doth flee;
on then, Christian soldiers,
on to victory!
Hell's foundations quiver
at the shout of praise;
brothers, lift your voices,
loud your anthems raise.

3 Like a mighty army
moves the Church of God;
brothers, we are treading
where the saints have trod.
We are not divided,
all one body we,
one in hope, in doctrine,
one in charity.

4 Crowns and thrones may perish,
kingdoms rise and wane,
but the Church of Jesus
constant will remain.
Gates of hell can never
'gainst that Church prevail;
we have Christ's own promise,
and that cannot fail.

5 Onward then, ye people!
Join our happy throng;
blend with ours your voices
in the triumph-song:
glory, laud, and honour
unto Christ the King!
This through countless ages
men and angels sing.

Sabine Baring-Gould 1834-1924

O Sacred Head Once Wounded

Bernard of Clairvaux was born at his father's castle near Dijon, France. He entered the first Cistercian monastery in 1113. He founded Clairvaux and became the first Abbot. Gerhardt found these words in *Salve Caput Cruentatum* and headed his 1656 version *To the Suffering Face of Christ*. It expresses the dying love of the Saviour. It tells of our debt to Him. The tune associated with this hymn was first published in 1601 and by 1656 became firmly associated with the hymn's lyric. Bach was an admirer and utilised it several times during his *St Matthew Passion*.

Passion Chorale

H. L. Hassler 1564-1612

1 O sa - cred head once wound - ed, with grief and pain weigh'd down, how
scorn - ful - ly sur - round - ed with thorns, thine on - ly crown! How
pale art thou with an - guish, with sore a - buse and scorn! How

does that vi-sage lan-guish which once was bright as morn.

2 O Lord of life and glory,
what bliss till now was thine!
I read the wondrous story,
I joy to call thee mine.
Thy grief and thy compassion
were all for sinners' gain;
mine, mine was the transgression,
but thine the deadly pain.

3 What language shall I borrow
to praise thee, heavenly friend,
for this thy dying sorrow,
thy pity without end?
Lord, make me thine for ever,
nor let me faithless prove;
O let me never, never
abuse such dying love!

4 Be near me, Lord, when dying;
oh, show thyself to me;
and, for my succour flying,
come, Lord, to set me free:
these eyes, new faith receiving,
from Jesus shall not move;
for he who dies believing
dies safely through thy love.

Paul Gerhardt 1607-76
(after Bernard of Clairvaux
1091-1153)
tr. James Waddell Alexander
1804-59

FATHER-LIKE HE TENDS & SPARES US;
WELL OUR FEEBLE FRAME HE KNOWS;
IN HIS HANDS HE GENTLY BEARS US,
RESCUES US FROM ALL OUR FOES:
PRAISE HIM! PRAISE HIM!
WIDELY AS HIS MERCY FLOWS.

"Praise, My Soul the King of Heaven" Verse 3

Praise, My Soul, the King of Heaven

Lyte's hymn has been much favoured for public occasion and ceremony. It was chosen by Queen Elizabeth II for her wedding to the Duke of Edinburgh. That day, 20 November 1947, was the centenary of Lyte's death.

Lyte's hymn is seen by numerous hymnologists as perfection. He based it on Psalm 103. He states that God's mercy and love remain constant and sure whatever the age and time. He sees God's love expressed in forgiveness. In the final verse he with the Psalmist summons the whole created universe to participate in an act of praise.

Regent Square

H. T. Smart 1813-79

1 Praise, my soul, the King of hea-ven, to his feet thy tri-bute bring;
ran-som'd, heal'd, re-stor'd, for-gi-ven, who like thee his praise should sing?
Praise him! Praise him! Praise him! Praise him! Praise the e-ver-last-ing King.

2 Praise him for his grace and favour
  to our fathers in distress;
  praise him, still the same for ever,
  slow to chide and swift to bless:
  praise him! Praise him! *(twice)*
  ·glorious in his faithfulness.

3 Father-like, he tends and spares us;
  well our feeble frame he knows;
  in his hands he gently bears us,
  rescues us from all our foes:
  praise him! Praise him! *(twice)*
  widely as his mercy flows.

4 Angels in the heights, adore him;
  ye behold him face to face;
  sun and moon, bow down before him;
  dwellers all in time and space,
  praise him! Praise him! *(twice)*
  praise with us the God of grace.

Henry Francis Lyte 1793-1847

O GENEROUS LOVE! THAT HE,
WHO SMOTE
IN MAN FOR MAN THE FOE,
THE DOUBLE AGONY IN MAN
FOR MAN SHOULD UNDERGO.

"Praise to the Holiest in the Height" Verse 5

Praise to the Holiest in the Height

This comes from Newman's *Dream of Gerontius*. It was first published in the Roman Catholic journal, *The Month in May,* June 1865. In 1868 it appeared in the appendix to *Hymns Ancient and Modern.* Cardinal Newman was born in the City of London. He became Vicar of St Mary's, Oxford and in 1845 he was admitted into the Roman Church.

The hymn has given much comfort to those near death. William Gladstone found it giving much assurance as he lay on his death-bed. Gordon found strength from its words as he faced death at Khartoum. It was sung at Newman's own funeral service.

Gerontius

J. B. Dykes 1823-76

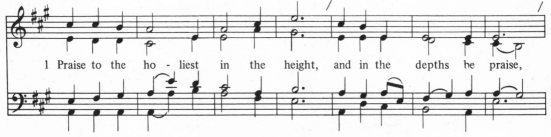

1 Praise to the ho - liest in the height, and in the depths be praise,

in all his words most won - der - ful, most sure in all his ways.

2 O loving wisdom of our God!
When all was sin and shame,
a second Adam to the fight
and to the rescue came.

3 O wisest love! that flesh and blood,
which did in Adam fail,
should strive afresh against their foe,
should strive and should prevail,

4 and that a higher gift than grace
should flesh and blood refine:
God's presence and his very self,
and essence all divine.

5 O generous love! that he who smote
in man for man the foe,
the double agony in man
for man should undergo;

6 and in the garden secretly,
and on the cross on high,
should teach his brethren, and inspire
to suffer and to die.

7 Praise to the holiest in the height,
and in the depth be praise,
in all his words most wonderful,
most sure in all his ways.

John Henry Newman 1801-90

Praise to the Lord, the Almighty

This splendid hymn with its so apt tune is based on Scripture, Psalm 103, 1-6 and Psalm 150. It first appeared in Neander's *Glaub und Liebesübung* of 1680. Three years later it appeared in Catherine Winkworth's *Chorale Book For England.* Neander came from Bremen. He was for a time Rector of the Latin School at Düsseldorf. The hymn was much liked by Friedrich Wilhelm III of Prussia.

The hymn speaks powerfully of the great activities of God. It calls on creation, on people to sound the triumphant Amen.

Lobe Den Herren

Stralsund Gesangbuch 1665

1 Praise to the Lord, the al - might-y, the King of cre - a - tion;

O my soul, praise him, for he is thy health and sal - va -

tion; all ye who hear, bro - thers and sis - ters, draw

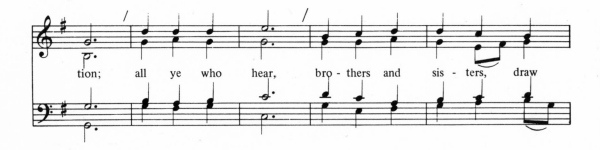

near, praise him in glad a - do - ra - tion.

2 Praise to the Lord, who doth prosper thy work and defend thee;
   surely his goodness and mercy here daily attend thee:
   ponder anew
   what the Almighty can do,
   if with his love he befriend thee.

3 Praise to the Lord, who, when tempests their warfare are waging,
   who, when the elements madly around thee are raging,
   biddeth them cease,
   turneth their fury to peace,
   whirlwinds and waters assuaging.

4 Praise to the Lord, who, when darkness of sin is abounding,
   who, when the godless do triumph, all virtue confounding,
   sheddeth his light,
   chaseth the horrors of night,
   saints with his mercy surrounding.

5 Praise to the Lord! Oh, let all that is in me adore him!
   All that hath life and breath, come now with praises before him!
   Let the Amen
   sound from his people again:
   gladly for aye we adore him.

Joachim Neander 1650-80
tr. Catherine Winkworth 1827-78 and others

Presence of the Lord

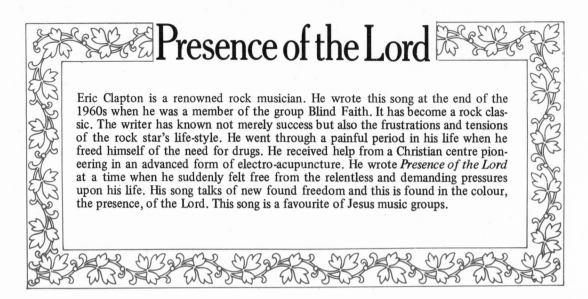

Eric Clapton is a renowned rock musician. He wrote this song at the end of the 1960s when he was a member of the group Blind Faith. It has become a rock classic. The writer has known not merely success but also the frustrations and tensions of the rock star's life-style. He went through a painful period in his life when he freed himself of the need for drugs. He received help from a Christian centre pioneering in an advanced form of electro-acupuncture. He wrote *Presence of the Lord* at a time when he suddenly felt free from the relentless and demanding pressures upon his life. His song talks of new found freedom and this is found in the colour, the presence, of the Lord. This song is a favourite of Jesus music groups.

Presence of the Lord

Eric Clapton

Slow

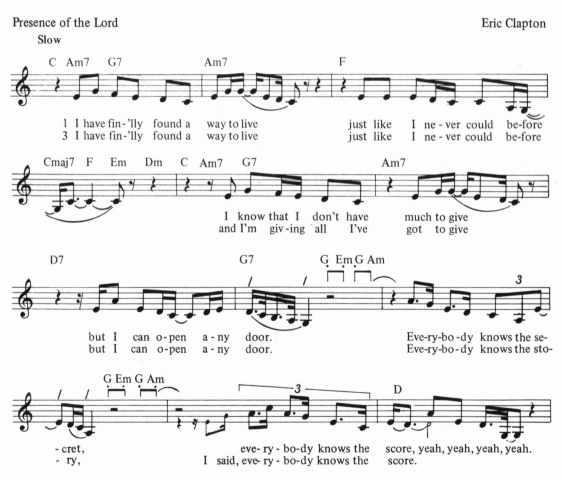

1 I have fin-'lly found a way to live just like I ne-ver could be-fore
3 I have fin-'lly found a way to live just like I ne-ver could be-fore

I know that I don't have much to give
and I'm giv-ing all I've got to give

but I can o-pen a-ny door.
but I can o-pen a-ny door.

Eve-ry-bo-dy knows the se-
Eve-ry-bo-dy knows the sto-

- cret,
- ry,

eve-ry-bo-dy knows the
I said, eve-ry-bo-dy knows the

score, yeah, yeah, yeah, yeah.
score.

REJOICE, THE LORD IS KING!
YOUR LORD & KING ADORE;
MORTALS, GIVE THANKS, & SING,
& TRIUMPH EVERMORE.

"Rejoice the Lord Is King" Verse 1

Rejoice the Lord Is King

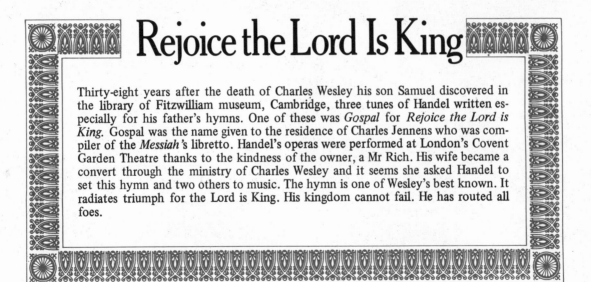

Thirty-eight years after the death of Charles Wesley his son Samuel discovered in the library of Fitzwilliam museum, Cambridge, three tunes of Handel written especially for his father's hymns. One of these was *Gospal* for *Rejoice the Lord is King*. Gospal was the name given to the residence of Charles Jennens who was compiler of the *Messiah's* libretto. Handel's operas were performed at London's Covent Garden Theatre thanks to the kindness of the owner, a Mr Rich. His wife became a convert through the ministry of Charles Wesley and it seems she asked Handel to set this hymn and two others to music. The hymn is one of Wesley's best known. It radiates triumph for the Lord is King. His kingdom cannot fail. He has routed all foes.

Gospal

G. F. Handel 1685-1759

1 Re - joice, the Lord is King! Your Lord and King a - dore; mor - tals, give thanks, and sing, and tri - umph e - ver more: *Lift up your heart, lift up your voice; re - joice; a - gain, I say, re - joice.*

(The refrain is sung after each verse)

2 Jesus the Saviour reigns,
  the God of truth and love;
  when he had purged our stains,
  he took his seat above:

3 His kingdom cannot fail,
  he rules o'er earth and heaven;
  the keys of death and hell
  are to our Jesus given:

4 He sits at God's right hand,
  till all his foes submit,
  and bow to his command,
  and fall beneath his feet:

5 He all his foes shall quell,
  shall all our sins destroy,
  and every bosom swell
  with pure seraphic joy:

6 Rejoice in glorious hope;
  Jesus the judge shall come,
  and take his servants up
  to their eternal home:

  We soon shall hear the archangel's voice;
  the trump of God shall sound, Rejoice!

Charles Wesley 1707-88

Ride On, Ride On in Majesty

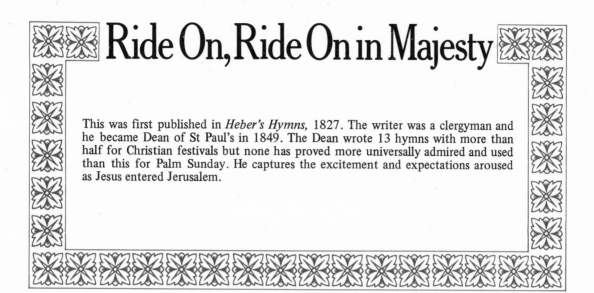

This was first published in *Heber's Hymns,* 1827. The writer was a clergyman and he became Dean of St Paul's in 1849. The Dean wrote 13 hymns with more than half for Christian festivals but none has proved more universally admired and used than this for Palm Sunday. He captures the excitement and expectations aroused as Jesus entered Jerusalem.

Winchester New

Musikalisches Handbuch 1690

1 Ride on, ride on in ma-jes-ty! Hark! all the tribes Ho-san-na cry; O

Sa-viour meek, pur - sue thy road with palms and scat-ter'd gar-ments strow'd.

2 Ride on, ride on in majesty!
In lowly pomp ride on to die;
O Christ, thy triumphs now begin
o'er captive death and conquered sin.

3 Ride on, ride on in majesty!
The wingèd squadrons of the sky
look down with sad and wondering eyes
to see the approaching sacrifice.

4 Ride on, ride on in majesty!
Thy last and fiercest strife is nigh;
the Father on his sapphire throne
expects his own anointed Son.

5 Ride on, ride on in majesty!
In lowly pomp ride on to die;
bow thy meek head to mortal pain,
then take, O God, thy power, and reign.

Henry Hart Milman 1791-1868

Rock of Ages

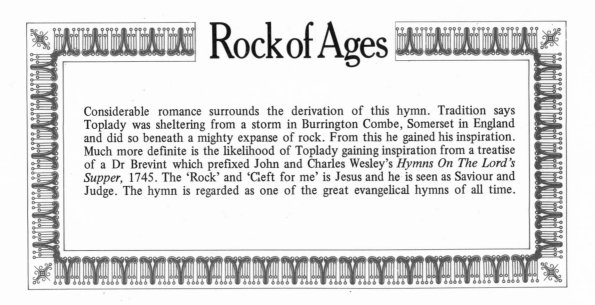

Considerable romance surrounds the derivation of this hymn. Tradition says Toplady was sheltering from a storm in Burrington Combe, Somerset in England and did so beneath a mighty expanse of rock. From this he gained his inspiration. Much more definite is the likelihood of Toplady gaining inspiration from a treatise of a Dr Brevint which prefixed John and Charles Wesley's *Hymns On The Lord's Supper,* 1745. The 'Rock' and 'Cleft for me' is Jesus and he is seen as Saviour and Judge. The hymn is regarded as one of the great evangelical hymns of all time.

Toplady

T. Hastings 1830

1 Rock of Ages, cleft for me, let me hide myself in thee; let the water and the blood, from thy riven side which flowed, be of sin the double cure, cleanse me from its guilt and pow'r.

2 Not the labours of my hands
  can fulfil the law's demands;
  could my zeal no respite know,
  could my tears for ever flow,
  all for sin could not atone:
  thou must save, and thou alone.

3 Nothing in my hand I bring,
  simply to thy cross I cling;
  naked, come to thee for dress,
  helpless, look to thee for grace;
  foul, I to the fountain fly:
  wash me, Saviour, or I die.

4 While I draw this fleeting breath,
  when my eyelids close in death,
  when I soar to worlds unknown,
  see thee on thy judgement throne,
  Rock of Ages, cleft for me,
  let me hide myself in thee.

        Augustus Montague Toplady

SILENT NIGHT, HOLY NIGHT.
SON OF GOD, LOVE'S PURE LIGHT:
RADIANCE BEAMS FROM THY HOLY
FACE
WITH THE DAWN OF REDEEMING
GRACE,
JESUS, LORD, AT THY BIRTH,
JESUS, LORD, AT THY BIRTH.

"Silent Night" Verse 3

Silent Night

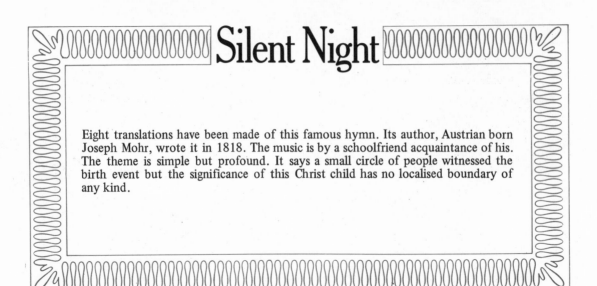

Eight translations have been made of this famous hymn. Its author, Austrian born Joseph Mohr, wrote it in 1818. The music is by a schoolfriend acquaintance of his. The theme is simple but profound. It says a small circle of people witnessed the birth event but the significance of this Christ child has no localised boundary of any kind.

F. Grüber 1787-1863
arr. P. Faber 1947—

Stille Nacht

2 Silent night, holy night.
Shepherds quake at the sight.
Glories stream from heaven afar,
heavenly hosts sing 'Alleluia!
Christ, the Saviour, is born!
Christ, the Saviour, is born!'

3 Silent night, holy night.
Son of God, love's pure light:
radiance beams from thy holy face
with the dawn of redeeming grace,
Jesus, Lord, at thy birth,
Jesus, Lord, at thy birth.

Josef Mohr 1792-1848
tr. J. Young 1820-85

Sing We the King

Charles Silvester Horne was the son of a Congregational minister and he followed in his father's footsteps. Among his charges was a prominent London chapel in the early years of this century. Known then and until recently as Whitefield's Tabernacle it is now the American Church in London. The hymn portrays the time when Jesus is King and the world finds true peace. Many people know the tune here used as the 'glory song' and it was much sung during the Moody-Sankey revival campaigns of the nineteenth century.

The Glory Song

C. H. Gabriel 1856-1932

1 Sing we the King who is com-ing to reign, glo-ry to Je-sus, the
Lamb that was slain, life and sal - va-tion his em-pire shall
bring, joy to the na-tions when Je - sus is King.

REFRAIN

(The refrain is sung after each verse)

2 All men shall dwell in his marvellous light,
races long severed his love shall unite,
justice and truth from his sceptre shall spring,
wrong shall be ended when Jesus is King.

3 All shall be well in his kingdom of peace,
freedom shall flourish and wisdom increase,
foe shall be friend when his triumph we sing,
sword shall be sickle when Jesus is King.

4 Souls shall be saved from the burden of sin,
doubt shall not darken his witness within,
hell hath no terrors, and death hath no sting;
love is victorious when Jesus is King.

5 Kingdom of Christ, for thy coming we pray,
hasten, O Father, the dawn of the day
when this new song thy creation shall sing,
Satan is vanquished and Jesus is King.

Charles Silvester Horne 1865-1914

Soldiers of Christ Arise

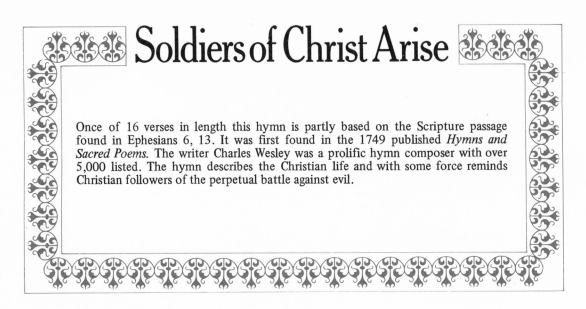

Once of 16 verses in length this hymn is partly based on the Scripture passage found in Ephesians 6, 13. It was first found in the 1749 published *Hymns and Sacred Poems*. The writer Charles Wesley was a prolific hymn composer with over 5,000 listed. The hymn describes the Christian life and with some force reminds Christian followers of the perpetual battle against evil.

From Strength To Strength

E. W. Naylor 1867-1934

1 Sol - diers of Christ, a - rise, and put your ar - mour on, strong in the strength which God sup - plies through his e - ter - nal Son; strong in the Lord of Hosts and in his might - y pow'r, who in the

strength of Je - sus trusts is more than con - quer - or.

2 Stand then in his great might,
with all his strength endued;
but take, to arm you for the fight,
the panoply of God;
that, having all things done,
and all your conflicts passed,
ye may o'ercome through Christ alone,
and stand entire at last.

3 Stand then against your foes,
in close and firm array;
legions of wily fiends oppose
throughout the evil day:
but meet the sons of night;
but mock their vain design,
armed in the arms of heavenly light,
of righteousness divine.

4 Leave no unguarded place,
no weakness of the soul;
take every virtue, every grace,
and fortify the whole:
indissolubly joined,
to battle all proceed;
but arm yourselves with all the mind
that was in Christ, your head.

Charles Wesley 1707-88

147

Stand Up, Stand Up For Jesus

Duffield was the son of a Presbyterian minister and himself became a much loved pastor. He said he was moved to write his hymns after listening to the dying words of a young clergyman, Reverend Dudley Tyng. Tyng died in tragic circumstances. His arms were torn from their roots when they became caught in the cogs of a horse-power machine. One of the last reported sentences of Duffield was spoken to a YMCA conference, 'Tell them to stand up for Jesus.' The hymn is a Christian call to duty and trust in the leader who is the King of Glory.

Morning Light

G. J. Webb 1803-87

1 Stand up, stand up for Je - sus, ye sol - diers of the cross; lift

high his roy - al ban - ner: it must not suf - fer loss. From

vic - t'ry un - to vic - t'ry his ar - my shall he lead, till

148

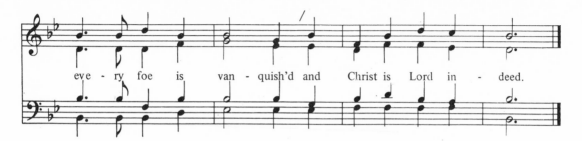

eve - ry foe is van - quish'd and Christ is Lord in - deed.

2 Stand up, stand up for Jesus!
The trumpet-call obey;
forth to the mighty conflict
in this, his glorious day!
Ye that are men, now serve him
against unnumbered foes;
let courage rise with danger
and strength to strength oppose.

3 Stand up, stand up for Jesus!
Stand in his strength alone:
the arm of flesh will fail you;
ye dare not trust your own.
Put on the Christian's armour,
and watching unto prayer,
where duty calls, or danger,
be never wanting there.

4 Stand up, stand up for Jesus!
The strife will not be long;
this day the noise of battle,
the next the victor's song.
To him that overcometh
a crown of life shall be;
he with the King of glory
shall reign eternally.

George Duffield 1818-88

Sweet Is the Work, My God, My King

Isaac Watts was born in Southampton, England, the eldest of nine children. His father, a schoolmaster, was twice imprisoned for his religious beliefs. Watts has been called the inventor of the hymn in the English language. Among many tributes is one from Josiah Condor who says, 'Watts was the first who succeeded in overcoming the prejudice which opposed the introduction of hymns into our public worship.' A monument to Watts is erected in Westminster Abbey.

This hymn is based on Psalm 92 and is one of many instances in which Watts paraphrases Scripture. It speaks of how good life is here yet sees even the splendours of the present pale into insignificance when the heavenly is known.

Eignbrook

The Hallelujah 1849

1 Sweet is the work, my God, my King, to praise thy name, give thanks and sing; to show thy love by morning light, and talk of all thy truth at night.

2 Sweet is the day of sacred rest,
  no mortal cares disturb my breast:
  oh, may my heart in tune be found,
  like David's harp of solemn sound!

3 My heart shall triumph in the Lord,
  and bless his works, and bless his word:
  thy works of grace, how bright they shine!
  How deep thy counsels, how divine!

4 And I shall share a glorious part,
  when grace has well refined my heart,
  and fresh supplies of joy are shed,
  like holy oil to cheer my head.

5 Then shall I see, and hear, and know
  all I desired and wished below;
  and every power find sweet employ
  in that eternal world of joy.

Isaac Watts 1674-1748

Tell Me the Old, Old Story

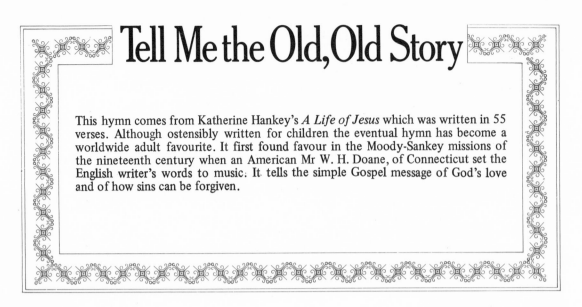

This hymn comes from Katherine Hankey's *A Life of Jesus* which was written in 55 verses. Although ostensibly written for children the eventual hymn has become a worldwide adult favourite. It first found favour in the Moody-Sankey missions of the nineteenth century when an American Mr W. H. Doane, of Connecticut set the English writer's words to music. It tells the simple Gospel message of God's love and of how sins can be forgiven.

Tell Me

W. H. Doane 1832-1916

1 Tell me the old, old sto - ry of un - seen things a - bove, of
Je - sus and his glo - ry, of Je - sus and his love.
Tell me the sto - ry sim - ply, as to a lit - tle child; for

152

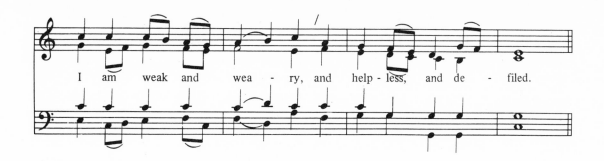

I am weak and wea - ry, and help - less, and de - filed.

REFRAIN

Tell me the old, old, sto - ry, tell me the old, old, sto - ry,

tell me the old, old sto - ry of Je - sus and his love.

(The refrain is sung after each verse)

2 Tell me the story slowly,
that I may take it in —
that wonderful redemption,
God's remedy for sin.
Tell me the story often,
for I forget so soon;
the early dew of morning
has passed away at noon.

3 Tell me the story softly,
with earnest tones and grave;
remember, I'm the sinner
whom Jesus came to save.
Tell me the story always,
if you would really be
in any time of trouble
a comforter to me.

4 Tell me the same old story
when you have cause to fear
that this world's empty glory
is costing me too dear.
Yes, and, when that world's glory
shall dawn upon my soul,
tell me the old, old story —
Christ Jesus makes thee whole!

Katherine Hankey 1834-1911

Tell Me the Stories of Jesus

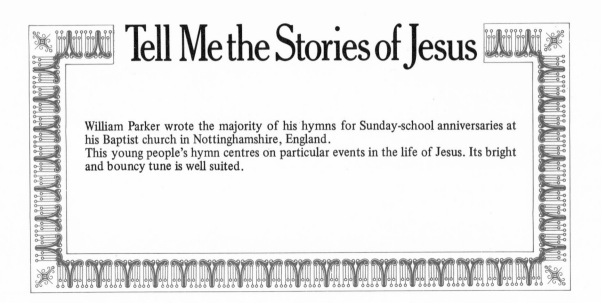

William Parker wrote the majority of his hymns for Sunday-school anniversaries at his Baptist church in Nottinghamshire, England.

This young people's hymn centres on particular events in the life of Jesus. Its bright and bouncy tune is well suited.

Stories of Jesus

F. A. Challinor 1866-1952

2 First let me hear how the children
   stood round his knee;
and I shall fancy his blessing
   resting on me:
words full of kindness,
   deeds full of grace,
all in the love-light
   of Jesus' face.

3 Tell how the sparrow that twitters
   on yonder tree
and the sweet meadowside lily
   may speak to me;
give me their message,
   for I would hear
how Jesus taught us
   our Father's care.

4 Tell me, in accents of wonder,
   how rolled the sea,
tossing the boat in a tempest
   on Galilee;
and how the Master,
   ready and kind,
chided the billows
   and hushed the wind.

5 Into the city I'd follow
   the children's band,
waving a branch of the palm-tree
   high in my hand;
one of his heralds,
   yes, I would sing
loudest hosannas!
   Jesus is King!

6 Show me that scene, in the garden,
   of bitter pain;
and of the cross where my Saviour
   for me was slain:
sad ones or bright ones,
   so that they be,
stories of Jesus,
   tell them to me.

William Henry Parker 1845-1929

Thank You

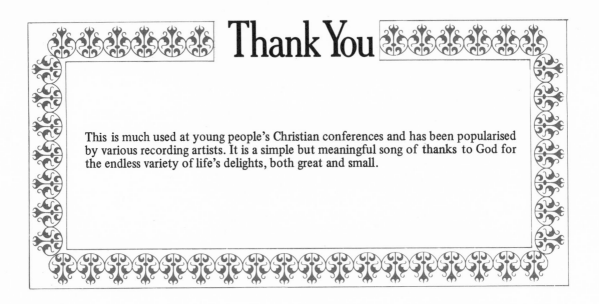

This is much used at young people's Christian conferences and has been popularised by various recording artists. It is a simple but meaningful song of thanks to God for the endless variety of life's delights, both great and small.

Thank You

Martin G. Schneider, arr. Colin Mayheather 1952—

1 Thank you for giv-ing me the morn-ing, / thank you for eve-ry day that's new, / thank you that I can know my wor-ries / may be shared with you.

2 Thank you for all my friends and brothers,
thank you for all the men that live,
thank you, for even greatest enemies
I can forgive.

3 Thank you for all my occupations,
thank you for pleasures great and small,
thank you for music, light, and gladness —
thank you for them all.

4 Thank you for many little sorrows,
thank you for every kindly word,
thank you, that everywhere your guidance
reaches every land.

5 Thank you, I see your word has meaning,
thank you, I know your Spirit here,
thank you because you love all people,
those both far and near.

6 Thank you, O Lord, for speaking to us,
thank you for telling us you care,
thank you, that you have come among us
bread and wine to share.

7 Thank you, O Lord, your love is boundless,
thank you that I am full of you,
thank you, you make me feel so glad
and thankful as I do.

Walter van der Haas,
Peter-Paul van Lelyveld and others

There Is a Green Hill Far Away

Inspiration for this extremely popular hymn came from the Apostles' Creed and the line 'Suffered under Pontius Pilate, was crucified, dead, and buried.' It was written at the bedside of a sick young person. The writer gives substance and answer to those who inquire why Jesus died. She talks of God's forgiveness. She speaks of how man can reclaim his original close relationship with God, and suggests the only possible response is the total giving of loving self. The event was for us.

Horsley

W. Horsley 1774-1858

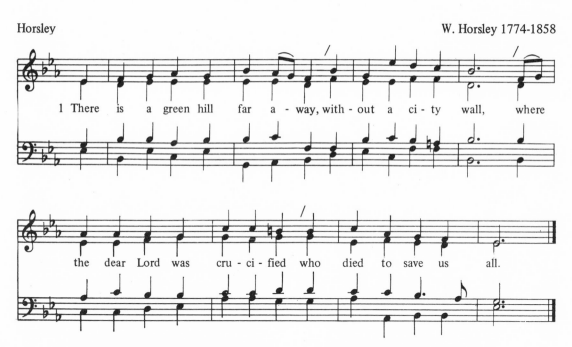

1 There is a green hill far a-way, with-out a ci-ty wall, where the dear Lord was cru-ci-fied who died to save us all.

2 We may not know, we cannot tell
what pains he had to bear;
but we believe it was for us
he hung and suffered there.

3 He died that we might be forgiven,
he died to make us good,
that we might go at last to heaven,
saved by his precious blood.

4 There was no other good enough
to pay the price of sin;
he only could unlock the gate
of heaven, and let us in.

5 Oh, dearly, dearly has he loved,
and we must love him too,
and trust in his redeeming blood,
and try his works to do.

Cecil Frances Alexander 1818-95

They'll Know We Are Christians by Our Love

This is arguably the most popular song amongst young American Christians. Slowly but surely through inclusion in a number of modern songbooks it is becoming known worldwide. It is very much a communal hymn. The song speaks of solidarity of believers and of love as the most expressive form of Christian commitment to others.

They'll Know We Are Christians by Our Love

Peter Scholtes

1 We are one in the Spi-rit, we are one in the Lord, we are one in the Spi-rit, we are one in the Lord, and we pray that all u-ni-ty may

one day be re - stored. *And they'll know we are Christ-ians by our love, by our*

REFRAIN

Em (Bm7) (Em) (Bm7) C (G) (C7) (Bm7) Em (+7)

love; yes, they'll know we are Christ-ians by our love.

(by our love.)

Am (Bm7) Em Am (Bm7) Em (Bm7) (Em)

(The refrain is sung after each verse)

2 We will walk with each other,
   We will walk hand in hand,
   we will walk with each other,
   we will walk hand in hand,
   and together we'll spread the news that God is in our land.

3 We will work with each other,
   we will work side by side,
   we will work with each other,
   we will work side by side,
   and we'll guard each man's dignity and save each man's pride.

4 All praise to the Father,
   from whom all things come,
   and all praise to Christ Jesus,
   his only Son,
   and all praise to the Spirit, who makes us one.

Peter Scholtes

LO! JESUS MEETS US, RISEN FROM
THE TOMB:
LOVINGLY HE GREETS US, SCATTERS
FEAR & GLOOM;
LET THE CHURCH WITH GLADNESS,
HYMNS OF TRIUMPH SING,
FOR HER LORD NOW LIVETH, DEATH
HATH LOST ITS STING.

"Thine Be the Glory" Verse 2

Thine Be the Glory

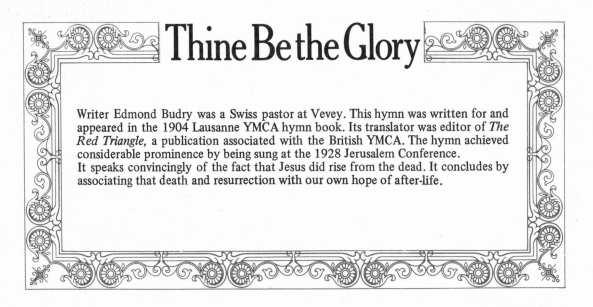

Writer Edmond Budry was a Swiss pastor at Vevey. This hymn was written for and appeared in the 1904 Lausanne YMCA hymn book. Its translator was editor of *The Red Triangle,* a publication associated with the British YMCA. The hymn achieved considerable prominence by being sung at the 1928 Jerusalem Conference.

It speaks convincingly of the fact that Jesus did rise from the dead. It concludes by associating that death and resurrection with our own hope of after-life.

Maccabaeus

Adapted from G. F. Handel 1685-1759

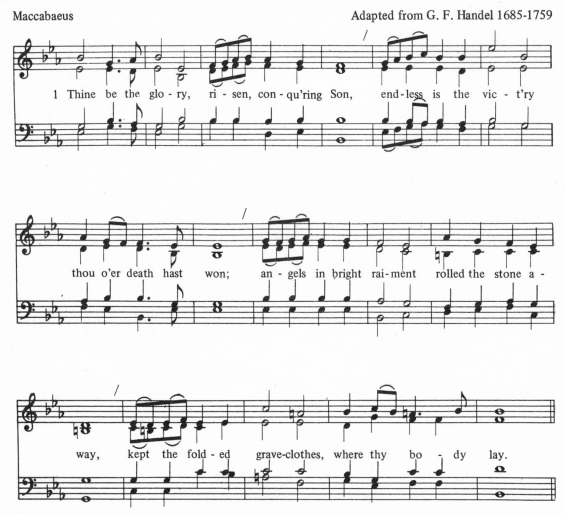

1 Thine be the glo-ry, ri-sen, con-qu'ring Son, end-less is the vic-t'ry thou o'er death hast won; an-gels in bright rai-ment rolled the stone a-way, kept the fold-ed grave-clothes, where thy bo-dy lay.

REFRAIN

Thine be the glo - ry, ri - sen, con - qu'ring Son,

end - less is the vic - t'ry thou o'er death hast won.

(The refrain is sung after each verse)

2 Lo! Jesus meets us, risen from the tomb;
  lovingly he greets us, scatters fear and gloom;
  let the Church with gladness hymns of triumph sing,
  for her Lord now liveth, death hath lost its sting.

3 No more we doubt thee, glorious prince of life;
  life is nought without thee: aid us in our strife;
  make us more than conquerors, through thy deathless love:
  bring us safe through Jordan to thy home above.

Edmond Louis Budry 1854-1932
tr. Richard Birch Hoyle 1875-1939

TO GOD BE THE GLORY! GREAT THINGS
HE HATH DONE!
SO LOVED HE THE WORLD THAT HE
GAVE US HIS SON;
WHO YIELDED HIS LIFE IN ATONEMENT
FOR SIN,
& OPENED THE LIFE-GATE THAT ALL
MAY GO IN.

"To God be the Glory" Verse 1

To God be the Glory

This Gospel hymn was first found in *Brightest and Best*, 1875. In common with many hymns which have become grouped under the general heading of the Gospel Call this sets out with clarity the basic message as found in Scripture, John 3, 16. There is the statement of what is offered and the invitation for response. As with many nineteenth century Gospel hymns there is expressed the belief that what is experienced here can only be infinitely greater in the after-life.

To God Be The Glory

W. H. Doane 1832-1916

1 To God be the glo-ry! great things he hath done! So loved he the world that he gave us his Son; who yield-ed his life in a-tone-ment for sin, and o-pen'd the life-gate that all may go in.

Praise the Lord! praise the Lord! Let the earth hear his voice! Praise the Lord! praise the

Lord! Let the peo - ple re - joice! Oh, come to the Fa - ther, through

Je - sus the Son: and give him the glo - ry! great things he hath done.

(The refrain is sung after each verse)

2 O perfect redemption, the purchase of blood!
to every believer the promise of God;
the vilest offender who truly believes
that moment from Jesus a pardon receives.

3 Great things he hath taught us, great things he hath done,
and great our rejoicing through Jesus the Son;
but purer, and higher, and greater will be
our wonder, our rapture, when Jesus we see.

Frances Jane van Alstyne 1820-1915

ATIME TO BE BORN, A TIME TO DIE;
A TIME TO PLANT, A TIME TO REAP;
A TIME TO KILL, A TIME TO HEAL;
A TIME TO LAUGH, A TIME TO WEEP.

"Turn, Turn, Turn" Verse 1

Turn, Turn, Turn

Famous American folk singer Pete Seeger has adapted the words of Ecclesiastes 3, 1-8. They cover the endless permutations of life. Numerous recorded versions of it have been made with the most famous being those by the American, West Coast group of the 1960s, The Byrds and trio Peter, Paul and Mary.

Turn! Turn! Turn!

Pete Seeger

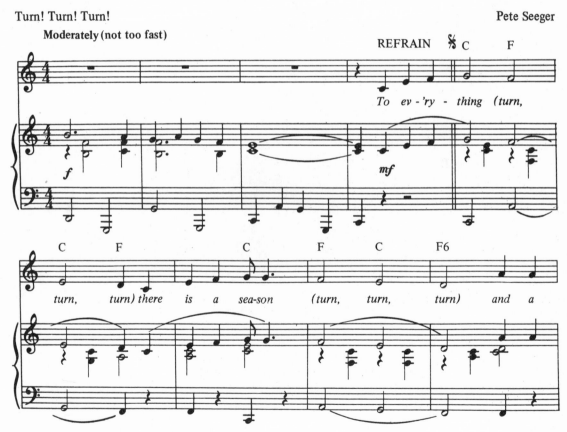

time to cast a-way stones, a time to gath-er stones to-ge-ther. *To ev-'ry*

3 A time of love, a time of hate; a time of war, a time of peace; a

REFRAIN

time you may em-brace, a time to re-frain from em-brac-ing. *To ev-'ry*

4 A time to gain, a time to lose; a time to rend, a time to sew; A time to love, a time to

172

hate; a time for peace, I swear it's not too late. *To ev-'ry*

REFRAIN

Words adapted from the Book of Ecclesiastes by Pete Seeger

We Love the Place, O God

William Bullock's hymn is much used on the occasions of church openings, anniversaries or dedications. It was written for a little church he built in the Trinity Bay area of Newfoundland. Bullock was a missionary and his familiarity with this area had come from considerable time spent there as a naval officer. During his time in Newfoundland he observed many people living in abject poverty without religious knowledge. He decided he would forgo his career and undertake religious work. His hymn expresses the joy of worship — particularly when it takes place in the house of God.

Quam Dilecta

H. L. Jenner 1820 - 98

1 We love the place, O God, where - in thine ho - nour dwells; the

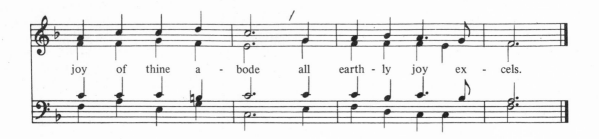

joy of thine a - bode all earth - ly joy ex - cels.

2 It is the house of prayer,
wherein thy servants meet;
and thou, O Lord, art there
thy chosen flock to greet.

3 We love the word of life,
the word that tells of peace,
of comfort in the strife,
and joys that never cease.

4 We love to sing below
of mercies freely given;
but oh, we long to know
the triumph-song of heaven.

5 Lord Jesus, give us grace
on earth to love thee more,
in heaven to see thy face,
and with thy saints adore.

William Bullock 1798 - 1874

bree - zes, and the sun - shine, and soft re - fresh - ing rain.

REFRAIN

All good gifts a - round us are sent from heav'n a - bove; then

thank the Lord, oh, thank the Lord, for all his love.

(The refrain is sung after each verse)

2 He only is the maker
  of all things near and far;
  he paints the wayside flower,
  he lights the evening star;
  the winds and waves obey him,
  by him the birds are fed;
  much more to us, his children,
  he gives our daily bread.

3 We thank thee then, O Father,
  for all things bright and good,
  the seed-time and the harvest,
  our life, our health, our food;
  accept the gifts we offer
  for all thy love imparts,
  and, what thou most desirest,
  our humble thankful hearts.

Matthias Claudius 1740-1815
tr. Jane Montgomery Campbell
1817-78

Were You There When They Crucified My Lord?

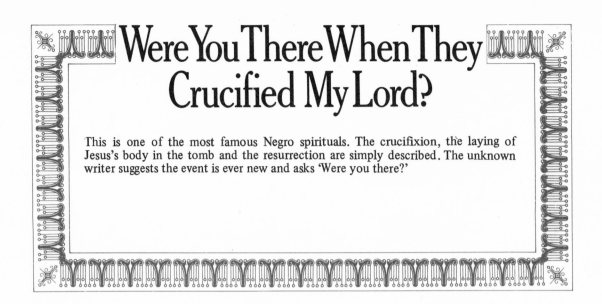

This is one of the most famous Negro spirituals. The crucifixion, the laying of Jesus's body in the tomb and the resurrection are simply described. The unknown writer suggests the event is ever new and asks 'Were you there?'

Were You There?

Negro Spiritual
arr. F. B. Westbrook 1903-75

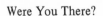

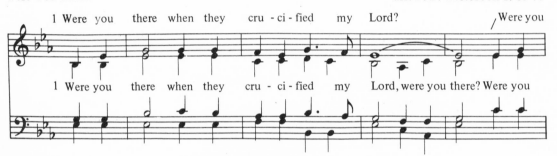

1 Were you there when they cru-ci-fied my Lord? Were you there when they cru-ci-fied my Lord, were you there? Were you

there when they cru-ci-fied my Lord? Oh! there when they cru-ci-fied my Lord, when they cru-ci-fied my Lord? Oh!

Some-times it cau-ses me to trem-ble, trem-ble,

trem - ble; were you there when they cru - ci - fied my Lord?

2 Were you there when they nailed him to the tree?
Were you there when they nailed him to the tree?
Oh! Sometimes it causes me to tremble, tremble, tremble;
were you there when they nailed him to the tree?

3 Were you there when the sun refused to shine? etc.

4 Were you there when they laid him in the tomb? etc.

5 Were you there when God raised him from the dead?
Were you there when God raised him from the dead?
Oh! Sometimes it causes me sing glory, glory, glory;
were you there when God raised him from the dead?

Traditional Negro Spiritual

What a Friend

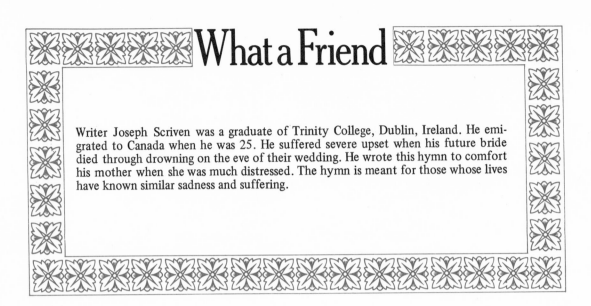

Writer Joseph Scriven was a graduate of Trinity College, Dublin, Ireland. He emigrated to Canada when he was 25. He suffered severe upset when his future bride died through drowning on the eve of their wedding. He wrote this hymn to comfort his mother when she was much distressed. The hymn is meant for those whose lives have known similar sadness and suffering.

What a Friend

C. C. Converse 1832-1918

1 What a friend we have in Je - sus, all our sins and griefs to bear!

What a pri-vi-lege to car-ry ev-'ry-thing to God in prayer!

Oh, what peace we of-ten for-feit, Oh, what need-less pain we bear,

all be-cause we do not car — ry ev-'ry-thing to God in prayer!

2 Have we trials and temptations?
   Is there trouble anywhere?
   We should never be discouraged:
   take it to the Lord in prayer.
   Can we find a friend so faithful,
   who will all our sorrows share?
   Jesus knows our every weakness:
   take it to the Lord in prayer.

3 Are we weak and heavy-laden,
   cumbered with a load of care?
   Precious Saviour, still our refuge:
   take it to the Lord in prayer.
   Do thy friends despise, forsake thee?
   Take it to the Lord in prayer;
   in his arms he'll take and shield thee,
   thou wilt find a solace there.

Joseph Medlicott Scriven 1820-86

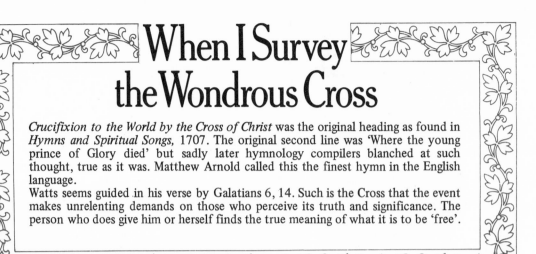

When I Survey the Wondrous Cross

Crucifixion to the World by the Cross of Christ was the original heading as found in *Hymns and Spiritual Songs,* 1707. The original second line was 'Where the young prince of Glory died' but sadly later hymnology compilers blanched at such thought, true as it was. Matthew Arnold called this the finest hymn in the English language.

Watts seems guided in his verse by Galatians 6, 14. Such is the Cross that the event makes unrelenting demands on those who perceive its truth and significance. The person who does give him or herself finds the true meaning of what it is to be 'free'.

Rockingham

Adapted by E. Miller 1731-1807
From A Second Supplement to Psalmody in Miniature 1780

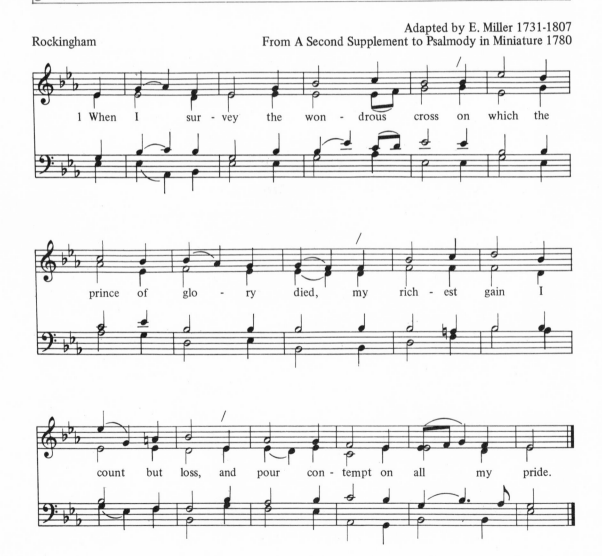

1 When I survey the wondrous cross on which the prince of glory died, my richest gain I count but loss, and pour contempt on all my pride.

2 Forbid it, Lord, that I should boast,
  save in the death of Christ, my God;
  the vain things that attract me most,
  I sacrifice them to his blood.

3 See, from his head, his hands, his feet,
  what grief and love flow mingled down;
  did e'er such love and sorrow meet,
  or thorns compose so rich a crown?

4 His dying crimson, like a robe,
  spreads o'er his body on the tree;
  then I am dead to all the globe
  and all the globe is dead to me.

5 Were all the realm of nature mine,
  it would be offering far too small;
  love so amazing, so divine
  demands my soul, my life, my all.

Isaac Watts 1674-1748

When We Walk with the Lord

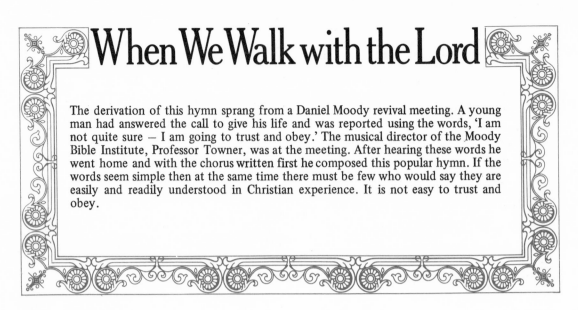

The derivation of this hymn sprang from a Daniel Moody revival meeting. A young man had answered the call to give his life and was reported using the words, 'I am not quite sure — I am going to trust and obey.' The musical director of the Moody Bible Institute, Professor Towner, was at the meeting. After hearing these words he went home and with the chorus written first he composed this popular hymn. If the words seem simple then at the same time there must be few who would say they are easily and readily understood in Christian experience. It is not easy to trust and obey.

Trust and Obey

D. B. Towner 1850-1919

1 When we walk with the Lord in the light of his word what a glo-ry he sheds on our way! While we do his good will, he a-bides with us still, and with all who will trust and o - bey.

Trust and o - bey, for there's no o - ther way to be

hap - py in Je - sus but to trust and o - bey.

(The refrain is sung after each verse)

2 Not a shadow can rise,
  not a cloud in the skies,
  but his smile quickly drives it away;
  not a doubt nor a fear,
  not a sigh nor a tear,
  can abide while we trust and obey.

3 Not a burden we bear,
  not a sorrow we share,
  but our toil he doth richly repay;
  not a grief nor a loss,
  not a frown nor a cross,
  but is blest if we trust and obey.

4 But we never can prove
  the delights of his love
  until all on the altar we lay;
  for the favour he shows,
  and the joy he bestows,
  are for them who will trust and obey.

5 Then in fellowship sweet
  we will sit at his feet,
  or we'll walk by his side in the way;
  what he says we will do,
  where he sends we will go —
  never fear, only trust and obey.

John Henry Sammis 1846-1919

Will Your Anchor Hold?

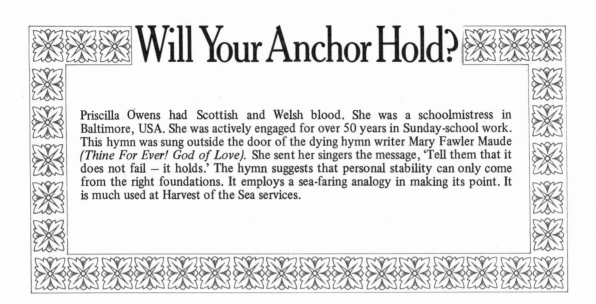

Priscilla Owens had Scottish and Welsh blood. She was a schoolmistress in Baltimore, USA. She was actively engaged for over 50 years in Sunday-school work. This hymn was sung outside the door of the dying hymn writer Mary Fawler Maude *(Thine For Ever! God of Love)*. She sent her singers the message, 'Tell them that it does not fail — it holds.' The hymn suggests that personal stability can only come from the right foundations. It employs a sea-faring analogy in making its point. It is much used at Harvest of the Sea services.

Will Your Anchor Hold?   W. J. Kirkpatrick 1838-1921

1 Will your an-chor hold in the storms of life, when the clouds un-fold their wings of strife? When the strong tides lift, and the ca-bles strain, will your an-chor drift, or firm re-main?

REFRAIN

We have an an-chor that keeps the soul

steadfast and sure while the billows roll; fastened to the Rock which

cannot move, grounded firm and deep in the Saviour's love!

(The refrain is sung after each verse)

2 Will your anchor hold in the straits of fear?
  When the breakers roar and the reef is near;
  while the surges rave, and the wild winds blow,
  shall the angry waves then your bark o'erflow?

3 Will your anchor hold in the floods of death,
  when the waters cold chill your latest breath?
  On the rising tide you can never fail,
  while your anchor holds within the veil.

4 Will your eyes behold through the morning light
  the city of gold and the harbour bright?
  Will you anchor safe by the heavenly shore,
  when life's storms are past for evermore?

Priscilla Jane Owens 1829-99

Acknowledgments

The publishers would like to thank the following copyright holders for permission to use their work. The following hymns and songs must not be reprinted from this or any other source without due permission from the appropriate copyright holder:

COME DOWN O LOVE DIVINE (page 28) Music, 'Down Ampney' by Ralph Vaughan Williams from the *English Hymnal*, by permission of Oxford University Press.

DAY BY DAY (page 36) Music and words, copyright © 1971 The Herald Square Music Co., 1619 Broadway, New York, N.Y. 10019, USA: International Copyright secured. All rights reserved. All rights for the United Kingdom, British Commonwealth (excluding Canada and Australasia and the Republic of Ireland) are administered by Carlin Music Corporation, 14 New Burlington Street, London W1X 2LR.

FOR ALL THE SAINTS (page 52) Music, 'Sine Nomine' by Ralph Vaughan Williams from the *English Hymnal*, by permission of Oxford University Press.

GOD OF CONCRETE, GOD OF STEEL (page 54) Music, 'New Horizons' by F. B. Westbrook, by permission of Oxford University Press. Words, the Rev. Richard G. Jones, Manchester.

HOW GREAT THOU ART (page 60) English words and music arranged by Stuart K. Hine. All rights in the Continental Americas are administered by Manna Music Incorporated, 2111 Kenmere Avenue, Burbank, California 91504.

JESUS THE LORD, SAID (page 72) Music, 'Yisu Ne Kaha', harmonized by F. B. Westbrook, by permission of Oxford University Press.

KUM BA YAH (page 74) Music, by permission of Paul Inwood.

LET US BREAK BREAD TOGETHER (page 78) Music, by permission of Paul Inwood.

LORD OF THE DANCE (page 82) Music and words by Sydney Carter. World use excluding USA: from *Green Print for Song*, by permission of Stainer & Bell Ltd. USA: by permission of Galaxy Music Corporation, New York.

THE LORD'S PRAYER (page 88) Music, by permission of Paul Inwood.

LOVE DIVINE ALL LOVES EXCELLING (page 90) Music, 'Hyfrydol', by permission of Paul Inwood.

MORNING HAS BROKEN (page 96) Music, 'Bunessan', harmonized by Martin Shaw; words by Eleanor Farjeon, from *Enlarged Songs of Praise*, by permission of Oxford University Press.

MY SONG IS LOVE UNKNOWN (page 98) Tune, 'Love Unknown', reprinted here by permission of the successor to the late Dr. Ireland.

ON A HILL FAR AWAY (page 114) Copyright © 1913 George Bennard. Copyright renewal 1941, The Rodeheaver Co. All Rights Reserved. Used by Permission.

PRESENCE OF THE LORD (page 130) Music and words, by permission of Throat Music Ltd, London.

SOLDIERS OF CHRIST ARISE (page 146) Tune, 'From Strength to Strength', reprinted by the kind permission of E. W. Naylor.

TELL ME THE STORIES OF JESUS (page 154) Music and words, by permission National Christian Education Council.

THANK YOU (page 156) Printed with the permission of Bosworth & Co Ltd, 14/18 Heddon Street, London W1R 8DP.

THEY'LL KNOW WE ARE CHRISTIANS BY OUR LOVE (page 158) Music and words by Peter Scholtes, by permission of F.E.L. Publications Ltd, 1925 Pontius Avenue, Los Angeles, California 90025.

THINE BE THE GLORY (page 162) Copyright © World Student Christian Federation. Used by permission.

TURN, TURN, TURN (page 170) Printed with the permission of Essex Music Limited, 4 Denmark Street, London WC2 for Melody Trails Inc., New York. All rights reserved.

WERE YOU THERE WHEN THEY CRUCIFIED MY LORD? (page 180) Music, 'Were You There', arranged by F. B. Westbrook, from *Hymns and Songs*, by permission of Oxford University Press.